MW01277943

Walk on Water

In the Light of Love
we are One

Daria 2018

Always I have been by your side...

from the moment your mother breathed you in

her womb, through the sands of time, until your

final ungrasping, and eternal release.

I am the guardian of the twilight, bridging and

reconciling separation.

I am the first – the birth of your Being.

I am the second - dancing in the patterns of choice.

Gaze into my mirror and you will see me in

everything.

I reflect all that is as I cast back a perfect image of

your heart.

I am One as the Divine Light illuminating every

step on the path of destiny.

Step out of the boat into the truth of Light and

walk with me.

Walk on Water

A journey into the eye of the storm

Daria Kathleen Sherman PhD

Published by: Heartland Publishing

Canton, OH 44718

Printed by Lulu Press in the United States of America

The information written in this book is not intended or implied to be a substitute for professional medical advice, diagnosis, or treatment. All content is for general information purposes only. Please see a medical professional if you need help with depression, illness, or have any concerns whatsoever.

First Edition

ISBN   978-1-387-98627-9

Dedicated to the 29-year-old version of myself

CONTENTS

Acknowledgements

Thank you my dear friend and exquisite artist Annemarie Schneider– owner of Creative Art Therapy. You captured the vision of this book, for it was through gazing at this painting that the words poured forth onto the pages. Facebook-CreativeArtTherapy@creativeart0815

Contributing writer Jeanne Grimes Brooks, author of "I Painted the Light", Shamanic Practitioner, Reiki Master, and Psychic Medium- www.willowwisewoman.com Thank you for the story of the Angel Ray Healing session. You eloquently described a beautiful and powerful encounter.

Stephanie, owner of a therapeutic healing business, thank you for talking with me about your powerful Touched by an Angel experience.

Contributing writer Diane L. Doll, Business Consultant www.ImagineLifeUnlimited.com Thank you for explaining how numerology has been a personal guidance system for decision making.

Contributing writer Barbara Braden Kelly, Reiki Master Teacher, owner of Circle of Life Reiki, Chi Lel Qigong Instructor. Barbarakamala1@aol.com Thank you for candidly describing that during a very difficult time, you were given the messages of Love and Joy.

Contributing writer Lisa Rockwell - Intuitive Energy Healer, Reiki Teacher, Spiritual Advisor, Intuitive Life Coach / Retreat Facilitator www.awakenoneness.com Thank you for describing one of your healing sessions with Mother Mary.

Prelude

Consistent effort every day will yield the results you are seeking. It is important to be steadfast no matter what. There will be more days than not that you won't feel like it. You will tell yourself, I will do this tomorrow or even later today. Most likely you won't, and another day will be gone. It is the nature of this post-modern life to consume all your moments. Therefore, carving out time to pause and reconnect with Source is necessary. It is all too easy to become distracted by the outer demands life presents. In less than five minutes from watching the news or reading Facebook, and Twitter posts one can become ensnared in the chaos. Even when you know this happens your mind will be too curious. A part of you doesn't want to miss anything, as if keeping abreast of all the drama is necessary.

There is a way to be aware of the world without getting tossed around in the storms. There are a few people who embody the state of absolute Peace in such a way that the storms of life can rage around them but cease to disturb them. This book offers several ideas through a 21-day process that will assist you to become one of those few people.

The gateway to begin a spiritual path is a personal one. The culture and beliefs you were raised through may become the platform for understanding the deeper meanings in your life. Yet the journey needs to be individualize in such a way that you seek Truth- Divinity- Love unencumbered. There are a multitude of resources available to give one a framework from which to work from. This book is one of them. When you have reached a point in your life where the limitation and restrictions of living in a boat are too painful you will be compelled to jump out into the water. Not yet knowing that you have everything within you to walk on the water you will if you know how, swim. After a while this singular effort of swimming across the deep waters you will become exhausted, some may even drown. The words expressed on these pages are a life raft to assist you on your journey. Yet like the boat, this too needs to be left behind for you to awaken to your destined path. I am sharing what worked for me. Only you can decide what truly inspires and awakens you to a life of alignment with Divine Presence. Each person emanates their own unique vibration frequency pattern. You and only you know what coherently propels your growth and alignment with life's highest calling.

When navigating the deep waters of life, recognize that there is more going on than what your physical senses and mind tell you. Because of fear that was programed into you, your experience may be of swimming in the ocean with sharks. You are not alone, and you never were. Trust in what you cannot yet see is guiding you to your destiny.

This book features stories that reveal a supernatural force of Love that is guiding our every step. After such experiences others report of being left with an indelible mark of calmness and peace. Even though their current life presentation is anything but peaceful after a 'touch by an angel' like encounter, they know that everything is going to be okay.

A balanced harmonious life expresses itself daily as growth and expansion. It is imperative that space within you is created for new growth to occur. If your daily schedule is already over packed, then it will be more difficult for something fresh and new to come in. The number one priority needs to be taking inventory of your own personal energy. Along with brushing your teeth daily; be aware of your energy vibration and detox your energy field when needed. Not being mindful or aware of one's own vibration allows for stagnation and the accumulation of dense and heavy energy. Life cannot bloom in a stressed-out body. Inspiration cannot take root. In the perfected state of a person the only thing that is present is Pure Possibility. This is the absolute alignment with God. Your soul is the light of God. Your body is the vehicle through which the light of God is expressed in this world. Your heart knows this truth. Your mind may conceptually recognize this truth but cannot abide there for very long. This is because your thoughts dwell in the past or future, both of which are conceptual constructs. Your thoughts are simply subjective ideas or theories. Because thoughts are subjective, in truth they are not based on empirical evidence, although you may argue against this presumption.

The endless network channels of communicated thought forms fill the spaces of creation. Yet behind, around, and though this endless chatter stillness speaks. Be still and listen to the quietness of this moment. Take in a deep breath and relax. Become one with the silence. There is peace here in a moment like this. Peace that cannot be achieved through thinking or doing, but from awareness; awareness of the totality of being. The continuous stream of thinking prevents you from ever fully relaxing into your life, and until you can relax into your life only then can you fully live your life. Only then can you veritably engage in expressing your divine nature which is who you truly are.

Breathe, pause, breathe, let go of your thinking and observe your breath. This will help you quiet your mind. In the silence, a space is created for true self-awareness to arise. A space is created for the life your soul is yearning for. When we become quiet we can hear the voice of God. Usually, at first it comes as a whisper. Other times the voice is revealed as a very harsh occurrence that shakes you out of your distorted version of reality. This isn't to punish you, rather to push you back into alignment with life's plan for you. And in those times when you failed to heed the whisper and loud voice you may have the experience of the rug being pulled out from under you, or even hit with a two by four. Cultivate a daily practice so that you become quiet enough to listen to the whisper. This is conscious living. This is deliberate and intentional which with consistency will yield the fruits of your efforts.

Life is filled with incredible moments perceived as highs and lows. By remaining open and centered and consistently committing to each experience as it arises verse our own personal judgments; the easier it will be to step out of conflict.

Have the willingness to begin each day as a new day. Simply accept all of life exactly as it is. Embrace all that you did and didn't do. It's time to let yourself and everyone else off the hook by recognizing everything for the blessing and miracle they are.

Your focus completely determines all your experiences. Move into a space of vibrational forgiveness as you feel your resistance to life situations fall away. In the release feel the freedom and peace.

Consciously connecting with Divine Source and being 100% responsible and accountable for your own personal energy places you in the eye of the storm. This is the place- space is the God space. To be aware of your inner reality is to align with Gods will for your life. Be conscious in every moment and allow that consciousness to set you and everyone you meet free. You are meant for so much more. Listen to the inner yearning of your heart. Follow the inner guidance that is wanting to move you into more than you could ever imagine. It only takes pure belief to walk on water. The writings in this book will help you to remember forming a bridge of belief. Now step out of the boat and walk with me.

Chapter 1

Feeling Stuck

Once upon a time which chronologically was approximately 25 ½ years ago (1992) I was living a very different life. Today the outer presentation holds similar patterns of structure, but the inner me is divergent to who I believed myself to be then. My memory of that stage of my life is like a dream in which the main character was a completely different person. Only a few threads, mainly the ones that connect me with my immediate family now remain. Those threads of time seemingly activate only when I interact with the family or friends I knew in years gone by. Through the process of transformation those personal relationships had to be redefined. Some adapted, many did not. Those that didn't, either fell away completely, or they continue to attempt to relate to me from who I was to them before.

I once recall a conversation with my son who had just completed a transformational program and was about to return home to a new normal with his family and friends. The results of an intensive program, his healing and growth and shifts were dramatic. He was unrecognizable even in physical appearance to the lost, troubled teen that had begun the program just 100 days prior. Would family and friends relate to him as he was in the present moment or would they hold him hostage to his past behaviors and mistakes?

I remember when my son was half way through his program thinking I just want my son back the way he was before all the trauma. I wanted my 10-year-old version of my child back. Recalling the times my son was young, happy and innocent, I was wishing for life to return to the way it was before. Fortunately, I was counseled and reminded that life is not retrogressive, it does not partake in yesterday. Life is now. My son was a teenager experiencing difficult hardships not the young boy that once needed me. I alleviated much of my own suffering when I realized and accepted life on life's terms. I had a teenager in rehab. Soon I would have a teenager nearly eighteen years in age that I would build a new relationship with. The new relationship lasted two years then through a terrible accident he died. Once again, I faced the wanting and longing to have my son back the way he was before he transitioned. I felt the irreconcilable ache for him to be physically alive. Truth be told in many moments I still do linger there.

It seems to be human nature to look back. Relationships deepen and build stronger bonds based on history created in moments shared together. A foundation establishes a shelter and protection. Yet if we solely relate through what is known from the past, the possibility for the evolution of growth and change is hindered. There is an energetic consequence of holding on to the past. The tighter you grasp to beliefs, memories and concepts of the past the less you are available to create and invite in something new. You will feel stuck on a perpetual wheel that gives you the experiences of the same as before.

By outward appearances, I look successful. I live in a nice condominium with a view of the lake from windows that extend from the floor to the ceiling. My weekends are booked six months out with work. I'm an author of 29 self-help books for children and adults. I am considered by many a thought leader and mentor who pioneers new ideas guiding others beyond the conventional. I even have the letters PhD with my name, expressing my expertise and educational credentials. At the local bank, I'm addressed as Dr. Sherman. I have deep meaningful relationships, and I enjoy relaxed playful days during the week with my granddaughter. My Face book posts give inspirational information from books or articles I have written, and feature photos of happy occasions with my family and friends.

While all these things are true, they felt like a façade; an outward appearance maintained to conceal a less pleasant or creditable reality. Internally I had struggled to reconcile a seemingly opposite exemplification. For what seemed like more years than not, my life has been accentuated with heart break and collateral damages. The process of a metaphorical death and rebirth has been painfully slow and because of which, my mind berated me. I held disappointment from decisions previously made and opportunities missed. I felt trapped and locked in a vibrational density that perpetuated a feedback loop of stuck energy. Regardless of the hours and weekend workshops for self-help, thousands of dollars spent on specialized trainings and post graduate studies, I chronically came up against an invisible wall. Some unknow force seemed to tether me. Unhappiness and disappointment were my private companions.

After a while my once dynamic spirit began to falter. Outwardly I continued to work hard delivering above and beyond for my clients. I took on meaningful projects, kept a clean and organized home, ate a healthy diet, meditated, and worked out at the gym. I recorded positive affirmations, attended spiritual gatherings and church services. I explored and processed infinite emotions. I volunteered, and I donated to charities. I did all the right stuff, yet the perceived fruits of these symbiotic choices delivered tenuous results. Inwardly the midlife stage of my life has been marked with extreme disappointment and evaporated ambitions, topped with a sprinkling of good old-fashioned guilt. I felt guilty because my discontent seemed unfounded. Who was I to dare to dream for something more than my current realities presentation? And on occasion I hosted a pity party as my mind dredged up previous woes. My list was extensive and impressively heart-wrenching. While I know the importance of validating and feeling the very real emotions, holding on to those emotions became gorilla glue stuck to my feet.

I really felt stuck. A definition that describes the word stuck is to put up with or persevere with something difficult or disagreeable. In the dictionary the synonyms used to describe "stuck" are; "put up with it · grin and bear it · keep at it · keep going · stay with it · see it through · see it through to the end · persevere · persist · carry on · struggle on · hang in there · soldier on · tough it out · peg away · plug away · bash on" (1) Giving reflection to the definition of the word stuck, I realize that I was living a pattern established in my earliest years of life through the belief systems of my family. The never give up mind set infiltrated the many ways in which I engaged with life. As a result, change was something I was reluctant to embrace. So, to usher in something new, the Universe/God seemingly pulled the rug out from under me. I didn't like that at all.

My individual experiences of discontent seem to be shared by many. The eighth Index – based on a survey of 2,215 young people aged 16 to 25 – reveals that many young people are feeling trapped by their circumstances, with almost a fifth (18%) saying they don't believe they can change their circumstances if they want to. (2)

Whether you are a young adult or midlife, there are times when you will feel stuck or trapped by circumstance. Possibly a decision, made years ago became the reasoning argument that led to other decisions. The results of those decisions keep you tethered by obligations and expectations. An extra ordinary life event, or choices another made that involved you may have actuated your current circumstances.

Why do we feel stuck? The truth is the average person doesn't live 76 years, they live the same year 76 times. Most people continue to make decisions based on fear or habit, even though those decisions accord less than desired results. Perhaps you're avoiding positive decisions because you fear change. You fear judgement and disapproval from others if you make the changes. Regardless the basis for unwanted circumstances, the feeling of discontent can be the signpost directing you to something better.

Crisis is usually the turning point in time when a difficult or important decision must be made. Examples of a crisis are the death of a loved one, job loss, life threatening medical diagnosis, accidents, victim of a crime, your spouse has an affair. As intensely disruptive and painful these incidents are they can be the catalyst for welcomed change.

The key words here are "can be". The potential is there. Even after experiencing the most arduous and un-bearable, one can move forward. However; many people become ensnared through personal identification with the traumas experienced. "He is survived by his wife, mother and children." "I am a cancer survivor". "She is a holocaust survivor". These sentences describe people in relationship to other people and events. They also keep one neatly tied to the other people and events, all which occurred in the past. The past and your relationship to it keeps you tethered in the same place. It also perpetuates a constant feed-back loop of tribulation. Stepping away from the suffering takes real courage. It takes willingness and inner work. Moving out of feelings of loss and heartbreak, victimization, apathy, depression and despair are exacting choices. Even on the darkest gloomiest days you must stand resolute and reach for inner freedom. With consistency and intention, you will experience the fruits of your efforts. Other times you will feel discouraged. When you feel discourage use this book as support. The good news is that right here, right now you have within everything to create anew a life filled with ease, joy and meaning.

Before doubt kicks in consider the cherry blossom buds on a cold often snowy spring morning. In Washington DC 2018, green buds appeared on February 25, and peak bloom occurred on April 5. (3) The buds didn't doubt warmer weather would arrive Paul Meyer, executive director of the Morris Arboretum at the University of Pennsylvania stated; "Cherries and other early spring blooming plants are highly variable as to when they bloom, and it's driven totally by warmth. During the winter, the closed cherry buds can tolerate below-freezing temperatures. But as things start to warm, they will break dormancy and they will start to swell." (4)

A caterpillar doesn't doubt its ability to transform into a butterfly. The Scientific America describes metamorphosis; "One day, the caterpillar stops eating, hangs upside down from a twig or leaf and spins itself a silky cocoon or molts into a shiny chrysalis. Within its protective casing, the caterpillar radically transforms its body, eventually emerging as a butterfly or moth." According to Scientific America the caterpillar digests itself, releasing enzymes to dissolve all its tissues. Certain highly organized groups of cells known as imaginal cells survive the digestive process. Before hatching, it grows an imaginal cell for each of the adult body parts it will need as a mature butterfly or moth. In some species, these imaginal cells remain dormant throughout the caterpillar's life. (5)

Like the imaginal cells in the caterpillar you have everything you need within as a potential. When the conditions are right, transformation is unequivocal. To create the conditions for your heart's desire you need to be willing to trust in your own Divinity. While your mind can give you a certain degree of understanding, your thoughts are bound in limitation established through disempowering beliefs. To experience and know real transformation one needs to break through the imagined boundaries born from false beliefs created by the mind. Even though the thoughts are imagined and often false their impact is physically real and influences a person's entire life.

Butterflies earn their wings through great effort. The process of change is often a painful one because it involves loss and sacrifice. If you are to transform beyond one form to another, a part of yourself needs to die. Letting go isn't easy especially when you are used to thinking in a certain way about your life and how you live it. Just as a caterpillar dies so that a butterfly can be born, release your old ideas and embrace a necessary change so that destiny can unite with you. If this is a transformational time for you, practice acceptance and trust that what you do not yet know is being made manifested for you. You know when you have reached a point where you can go no further in the same manner as before. Take a deep breath and release your grip.

There is a story of a baby prince who was stolen from his father the King. The King was one of the wealthiest and kindest Kings in all the land. The King searched in earnest for his son but couldn't find him. The baby prince grew into a young man. For 19 years he lived a life of a poor peasant in a family and community of other peasants. The King never gave up searching for his son the prince. Finally, one day the King received word that the prince was living with the peasants. The king dispatched his soldiers to go retrieve his son. The soldiers came to escort the son back home to the palace, which was a place of absolute splendor. However, the son didn't want to go, so the soldiers forced him to leave with them. As they made their journey to the castle the son cried in despair as he looked back at his village. The young prince only knew life as a poor peasant. He had no reference point for what a life as a prince was. He suffered and experienced emotional pain because he kept looking back at what he knew. He resisted his future because it was unknown.

It takes courage and faith to walk a new path into the unknown. The journey will be much easier if you pack lighter by releasing the past. Life is not retrogressive, it does not partake in yesterday, so withdraw your evocations. Before you call in your future take pause to access your mindset. If you are attached to previous unresolved experiences, those experiences may attract more of the same.

Chapter 2

Eye of the Storm

In a study on March 30, 2015 at Langone Medical Center stated, "Neuroscientists tracked neuronal activity in dendritic nerve branches in mice who were running forward and backward on treadmills. Screen images appeared as tiny "lightning bolts" in the dendrites. The "lightning bolts" patterns were tied to the strengthening or weakening of connections between neurons, hallmarks of learning new information. Additionally, separate patterns of lightning bolt-like activity in the dendrites of brain cells occurred. These lightning bolts triggered a chain-like reaction, which changed the strength of connections between neurons." (6) Hospitals use an electroencephalogram (EEG) as a test to evaluate the electrical activity in the brain. Brain cells communicate with each other through electrical impulses. (7) The average mind is like a storm. By Googling images of electrical impulses in the brain you will see that when thoughts occur the brain lights up like a lightning storm.

Daily through Facebook feeds, internet, and news channels we are bombarded with information; most which is chaotic, and fear based. We live in a perpetually hectic world. There are so many things that pull our attention away from what we really need to be focusing on in every moment. There is a continuous whirlwind of distractions eroding precious time. The lazy peaceful days of drinking lemonade on a front porch swing are distance memories known only to a few elders. How can one become disengaged from the constant storms of life without becoming disconnected? How do you become fully present and available for every moment of your life yet remain peaceful? Is it possible to be fully at peace during so many storms?

Regardless our attempts to maintain a constant or status quo nothing ever stays the same. Change is a constant. How we respond to change, and how we evolve in the presence of life's inner yearning, is determined through how we receive grace. Grace aligns you to the harmonic patterns of the universes. Through Grace you begin to flow with the current of life rather than against it. Paradoxically, you flow with life when you make the decision to be still and abide in peace. You will know you are there when the chaos around you ceases to disturb you. When you embody absolute wholeness and peace, everything around you will entrain to that vibration. When Jesus walked the earth, he embodied absolute peace.

In the Bible Mark 4: 36-41 it is written: "And leaving the crowd, they took him with them in the boat, just as he was. And other boats were with him. And a great windstorm arose, and the waves were breaking into the boat, so that the boat was already filling. But he was in the stern, asleep on the cushion. And they woke him and said to him, "Teacher, do you not care that we are perishing?" And he awoke and rebuked the wind and said to the sea, "Peace! Be still!" And the wind ceased, and there was a great calm. He said to them, "Why are you so afraid? Have you still no faith?" And they were filled with great fear and said to one another, "Who then is this, that even the wind and the sea obey him?" (8)

When the world is a whirlwind of storms evoking chaos around you, and it feels like everything you hold dear is crumbling, there is a space that fear, heartbreak, and discouragement can never touch. This space is Love absolute. Jesus embodied the perfected Love absolute. Love absolute isn't a place separate from you. This fullness of Love is always ever-present. This Love is in every drop of rain, on every leaf, and in the hearts of every person. The only obstacle to experience this Love is the minds mental chatter and un-conscious beliefs that one is unworthy to receive such unconditional and Divine Love. To experience peace, be still and know. Make the time to journey inward. When you ground in stillness, you reside in the eye of the storm. Stillness is a state of Being that is beyond the chaos and movements of life. Providence, the Universe, God, Life, whatever you want to label such makes no difference. There is an indelible conscious presence that is guiding you through every area of your life. The invitation is always there. The conditions now on this planet are ripe for you to come back home and reside in as the embodiment of Divine Absolute. Walk away from the chaos of the outer world. This is important.

What do I mean when I write for you to come back home? Home is accessed by calling your awareness inward. The journey home is a journey inward. Through consistent effort you will retrain yourself to abide in Peace, not just for a few minutes rather as a way of life. The alignment of Peace absolute is Power absolute. This is the state of the masters. It is the offering from Jesus when he declared; "Peace be with you." It is because Jesus embodied this state of peace that the miraculous, the supernatural were his normal. In the bible John 6: 18-21 states; "A strong wind was blowing, and the waters grew rough. When they had rowed about three or four miles, they saw Jesus approaching the boat, walking on the water; and they were frightened. But he said to them, 'It is I; don't be afraid.' Then they were willing to take him into the boat, and immediately the boat reached the shore where they were heading." (9) Prior to this remarkable occurrence the bible Matthew 14:22-23 discusses; "Immediately Jesus made the disciples get into the boat and go on ahead of him to the other side, while he dismissed the crowd.

After he had dismissed them, he went up on a mountainside by himself to pray." (10)

Many masters exemplify a powerful state of presence. If you happen to be graced by a personal encounter with such a sage you will feel their abiding peace and the power that only such peaceful states can procure. They are in the world but not of the world. While the chaos, and madness pushes others around these masters are untouched because they stand in the eye of the storm. For it is in this space of stillness, alinement with Truth is actualized. The light of Truth dissolves fear.

Years ago, I dreamed of a man standing in the narthex of a great cathedral. He was a simple looking Asian man wearing black pants and a solid white shirt. I was standing next to him but wanted to walk into the main church were the congregation was gathering. The man didn't say anything but looked at me with the expression on his face saying, "you are not going in there, are you?" I hesitated and then a powerful wind blew into the church causing horrible destruction. It took every ounce of strength for me not to be blown into the storm. I looked over at the Asian looking man standing beside me. Not one hair on his body was moved or affected by this powerful wind that was destroying everything and everyone. Swirls of chaos moved around him yet every part of his being and physical form was completely untouched.   As I awakened the following morning I looked outside my window to the trees. Buds where emerging promising new life, and new beginnings. A part of me knew that change was being ushered in. My current realities presentation was tumultuous. I walked around beaten down and lifeless. Inside my spirit was crying out for a future life that needed to be lived. Yet I had no idea what that was supposed to be. I only knew that if I stayed in a destructive marriage, I would not live long.

Recalling the dream, I was enthralled not by the stormy winds but by the man standing calm, resolute, and untouched. Several months later I was invited to an introduction presentation on Qigong. As fate may have it, the level one classes where taught in the auditorium of a church, and the teacher, Master Hao was the man in my dream. In this prophetic dream, Master Hao was standing in the narthex of a church. The narthex is an architectural element typical of early Christian and Byzantine basilicas and churches consisting of the entrance or lobby area, located at the west end of the nave, opposite the church's main altar. Traditionally the narthex is a part of the church building; yet is not considered part of the church proper. In my dream, Dr. Hao was in the church but not part of the storm. His message is that by becoming centered in your power, you will remain peacefully unaffected by the traumas of the world around you. Guides and teachers both physical and from the realms of spirit are communicating with you. They are the keepers of light illuminating your path. Choose to live your Highest calling. When that choice is made with the heart, heaven and earth will move in fulfillment of your souls yearning.

Chapter 3

Energy Leaks

One of the teachings I learned while staying at Leela Mata's Peaceful Valley Ashram addressed Spiritual energy leaks. The milk of a lioness is so potent that no container can hold it except one made from pure gold. If the golden vessel has impurities, the milk will eat through the vessel like acid at the points of impurities resulting in the milk draining out. This metaphor is an important one for anyone embarking on a spiritual practice. If you have too many energy leaks, then the spiritual energy (shakti) that is generated through your meditation practice will simply leak away again.

Notice that after attending an empowering weekend retreat involving spiritual practices, quiet reflection, meditation and inspirational lectures you return home refreshed and renewed only to feel tired and stress within a few days of your regular routine. This common occurrence is do to energy leaks.

The number one energy leak is caused by exhaustion from multi-tasking. Statistics reveal that the fast-spaced lifestyle leaves minimal down time for relaxation and fun. An exhausted body and mind is depleted of its life force prana. As a result, the aura which is your first line of defense, thins and becomes riddled with holes.

An authentically balanced life for ultimate health would consist of a schedule of four hours off a day, one full day off a week, and one full weekend off a month, and three full weeks off a year. This time off needs to be unscheduled time free of preplanned activities unless those activities are playful, relaxing and connecting with loved ones. Another huge energy leak is the result of excessive emotions. If you are reacting to any outside disturbances, then you are losing energy to those disturbances. A powerful balanced person is one who responds to life situations verses react to them. This is an important distinction. One who responds does so from a balanced centered state of Presence. The reactive person is pushed around on the waves of the storms. The reactive person invests a lot of their personal energy into many things that emotionally trigger them, resulting in almost immediate depletion of personal energy.

It is quite common that after a period a deep emotional stress that is beyond the ordinary a person will become physically ill. Once the body is fighting an infection it is temporary much weaker.

It takes extra life force energy to fight disease and reestablish homeostasis.

Most of the people on this planet vibrate at a frequency that weakens them. This is because the majority dwell in the conceptual world of the mind stressing about the future and regretting the past. Strongly held beliefs, fixed polarized opinions weaken the physical body and create energy leaks.

Candace Pert, PhD, author of Molecules of Emotion, create a new branch of science called "Psychoneuroimmunology". PNI unites neuroscience, immunology and endocrinology and their associated glands and organs into a multidirectional communication network. Neuro peptides are the messengers that link these systems of the body together. (10) Pert's research reveals new scientific understanding of the power of our minds and our feelings to directly and profoundly affect our health and well-being. The brain is integrated into the body at a molecular level therefore we are one system. Emotions are energy, so when we think a thought and add emotion to it we are imprinting and programming the very atoms within and around us.

Unhealthy relationships are huge energy leaks, especially if one hangs on to a relationship that is past it's 'expiration date' out of fear or attachment. Relationships that are unclear about the level of commitment, or unclear regarding boundaries drain the life force quickly. When one person is giving more to the relationship than the other, the synergy needed for both individuals to thrive is disconnected. The feelings of compression, exhaustion, and depression are indicators of energy leaks do to a relationship that is unevenly yoked.

In general people talk too much. It seems some are afraid of the silence and feel the need to fill the gaps. Unconscious talking, excessive talking and gossip create an energy drain both by the talker and the one listening.

Everything is energy, and everything vibrates. There is a constant energetic adaptation going on with everything. If you're around someone in a bad mood long enough they will start to bring your energy down and you will bring theirs up.

The growing amounts of EMF's are negatively impacting everything. This is because an excessive imbalance has been created. Kaitlyn Keyt, owner of Vibes Up states; "Cell phones, computers, microwaves have positive ions (+) must complete or balance themselves by collecting (-) negative ions. Our electronics put out massive positive ions (+) and as long as there are plenty of (-) negative ions (nature) around you, the (+) will 'feed' on the nature to complete themselves. When it does not have the negative ions around (nature) it will go for the next best thing and literally etch away at your bodies causing even more imbalances, mental, physical and emotional." (11)

I studied the Eastern Healing Arts with a powerful Qigong Master.   One of the most important concepts he taught was "holding your power." Through various exercises, meditations and teachings on the energy body – specifically the meridians, I learned to work with Qi.   Qi is life force energy. Through daily practice one can build up a store house of this prana. This Qi should be held quietly and not wasted on parlor tricks to impress others with the energy. The moment anything is expressed in the physical it begins to die. That is a fundamental truth of all physical manifestations. After a meditation practice, hold the fruits of that practice close. Spend more time in silent awareness.   Live your life in such a way that the good high vibrations created from your practice stay with you and continue to accumulate. Embody the state of wholeness and fullness. After you are filled the rest of the world can benefit from the overflow.

Chapter 4

Fullness of Love

It is time to shift the way in which you are relating to your life and the world around you. This probably hasn't occurred to most people but we as individuals are living as a past memory or past version of ourselves. We are trapped in the past expressions of ourselves because of our minds. We are living a conceptual reality instead of the actual reality. How does one move beyond this quandary? How do we align with our highest calling? Begin by answering the call. Your highest calling doesn't have a ceiling. This means that as you evolve so to your highest calling evolves. Ask yourself, "what is the highest vibrational representation of me that I can be?" Made in the likeness and image of the Divine you are infinite. Therefore, who you are is not a stagnant identity rather you are the dance of life. People are so fearful of giving up their individual identity. Yet identity is just a mental construct. The dictionary describes identity as "the distinguishing character or personality of an individual: individuality and the relation established by psychological identification." (22) Psychological references for "identity" are mental and emotional states of being and as such are abstract. Abstract means symbolic or theoretical. Defining the self by identity alone overlays the life experiences in limitation. You are Spirit forever unfolding, unbounded, eternal and free.

Live in wander and question. Recognize that everything of physical form is a memory. You are relating to a memory of you. Everything around you, your life, and interactions are experienced because of memory. When you gaze upon the lamp on your desk. Your mind immediately gives you the word lamp. How do you know it is a lamp? You know because you learned the name previously, most likely as a young child. Look at the lamp on your desk. Can you look at it without knowing that it is a "lamp"? It is quite challenging to not have the mind give a continuous narrative of your life. I'm not suggesting that you embark on a strict regimen of meditation to quiet the mind. However, a daily practice will reduce stress and quicken your evolution into higher states of awareness. Simply notice that this is what the mind does. Remind yourself that you are conceptually perceiving a past construct.

Hermeticism, is a religious, philosophical, and esoteric tradition based primarily upon writings attributed to Hermes Trismegistus. The first of the seven hermetic principles are Mentalism. The all is mind.

"Reality underlying all the outward manifestations and appearances which we know under the terms of "The Material Universe"; the "Phenomena of Life"; "Matter"; "Energy"; and, in short, all that is apparent to our material senses is spirit which is unknowable and undefinable, but which may be considered and thought of as a universal, infinite, living mind. It also explains that all the phenomenal world or universe is simply a Mental Creation of the All, subject to the Laws of Created Things, and that the universe and in its parts or units, has its existence in the Mind of the All, in which Mind we "live and move and have our being." (23)

Basically, we exist in the mind of God which is infinite. Yet we have the illusional perspective that we are separate. The separation experience gives birth to the concept of time and limitation.

Jesus, Buddha, and many ascended masters know that they and Infinite/God are One. You exist in the mind of God. Your physical body, your thoughts, emotions, your entire life... exists within You. The process to embody a perception of knowing the truth of those two previous statements is a daily one.

Samadhi is the state were the mind becomes still. Samadhi is the absorption of the self. It is the state where the individual mind becomes absorbed in Divine Mind/ God. The individual identity that the mind has held is integrated into the eternal "I" of God. All aspects of the mind, heart, personality move into complete harmony and union with Divinity. Samadhi is transcendental consciousness in activity and stillness. This is the state of living with one foot in the world and one foot out. This is the state of absolute, of divine union that is quoted from Jesus in prayer. In the bible, John 17: 20-22 are quotes from Jesus in prayer, "My prayer is not for them alone. I pray also for those who will believe in me through their message, that all of them may be one, Father, just as you are in me and I am in you. May they also be in us so that the world may believe that you have sent me. I have given them the glory that you gave me, that they may be one as we are one." (24)

Meditation on the Divine and aligning with the Infinite Mind inaugurates imprints of Samadhi. As you return repeatedly through meditation you begin to experience the Divine connection in your waking consciousness. The more we abide in the state of pure presence the more the illusion of ego falls away. This makes it possible to step out of experiences of lack and limitation. One will begin to navigate the world from an expansive place of connection.

Meditation is about 'releasing thought'. This opens a space for your mind and body to resonate at your true vibrational level. By pausing and focusing on your breathing only, you're not introducing new thoughts into your mind. In releasing thoughts, resistance dissolves. When resistance is gone, everything you desire starts to move more quickly into your life. A 15-20-minute mind-break will allow this space of non-resistance to expand throughout your day the more you stick with a meditation practice the more benefits you will receive. Meditation is the foundation to all spiritual practices. If you are committed to your spiritual growth then it is vital to take time to meditate daily.

Divine absorption is the solution to ALL things. Therefore, this needs to be the soul reference point for living. Imagine immersing yourself in Light. Light dissolves all density. Every thought and image that you carry that holds an emotional charge is dense stuck energy. Divine Light illuminates all the areas that are holding you back, keeping you stuck. Are you willing to look? Are you ready to unconditionally love every part of you and your life? Are you ready to step your toes into the water?

If you become quiet enough in your mind, you begin to feel the expansive Love in everything. The fullness of Love is always ever-present. This Love is in every drop of rain, on every leaf, and in every grain of sand. The only obstacle to experiencing this Love it the minds mental chatter and un-consciousness beliefs in unworthy.

For most people their habit of compulsive thinking is so pervasive that they lose sight of the fact that they are nearly always thinking. Life is nothing more than passing experiences. Your thoughts are just one more category of things that you experience. Like any experience they arise in your awareness, they have a certain texture and they give way to something else. You observe your thoughts just as you can observe objects. Have you ever asked yourself, "Who is the Observer of these thoughts in my mind?"

Chapter 5

When Heaven Speaks

There are signposts illuminating the next steps on your life journey, for we are not meant to navigate this life journey alone. However, most people are immersed in daily survival of living in the matrix that they miss the messages. Yet the guidance is always there. Often at key pivotal moments in our lives we have experienced contact with beings of light, angels, ascended masters, and crossed-over loved ones who are now our guardians. The realms of spirit are without the restriction of physical form, therefore; their expeditious vibrations procure instant manifestations. At will they shift and step down their vibrational state in a spiral pattern into multitudinous realities. One reality is this physical one. When the two worlds meet a bridge of light is irrevocably formed. The supernatural experiences are imprinted in our hearts. Sometimes these experiences have such an impact that they change the course of our lives. Other times messages from Spirit are soothing reminders that we are loved and that we are not alone.

In life there are times when a breakdown of epic and unmanageable proportions occurs. This breakdown can open a person up to communion with heavenly beings. Other people who have no inner desire to seek something more; and are living out an ordinary life, have experienced what can only be explained as a Grace that saturates them with illuminated revelations. .

The experiences of the mystical encounters happen more frequently than documented. Numerous people who have described near death experiences revealed a communion with a luminous presence. Others discourse how in a profound, sublime experience they have felt, even seen a Holy Light along with religious figures such as Jesus, Mother Mary, Buddha or Quan Yin. The impact of such experiences convinced them that there is a guiding presence in their lives.

The Holy Bible gives revelations to the light called forth by God in the beginning of creation. Numerous accounts reveal the light portrayed as the Holy Spirit and in conjunction with visitations by angels or spirit guides.

Deep meditation and prayers have been practiced for centuries to attain a mystical divine union. Historical accounts discuss transformational moments of encounters with a quintessence, giving revelation to a personal divine holy communion that is possible for everyone. Various religions and cultures have unique interpretations describing a fundamental creative God force. The Holy light is both God and the creative force Christians call the Holy Spirit.

Historical works and numerous accounts of current day revelations from varied sources, cite the powerful moments transpired, elevating a person into the truth of oneness, or presence with Divinity. These experiences even if known for but a moment, can irrevocably change the course of one's life. In the moments of deep surrender and vibrational alignment, oneness is once again remembered.

The story of the transfiguration of Jesus records a pivotal moment when Jesus accompanied by three apostles hiked up to a mountain. Upon reaching the mountain's summit, the apostles witness Jesus shining with blazing bright rays of light from within and around him. This story isn't unique. Many religious discourses site the presence of a light emanating from within and around prophets, saints and holy messengers.

Meeting a Holy Messenger

Jeanne Grimes, author of the book "I Painted the Light" discusses in her book a very personal and powerful experience which she describes as meeting a holy messenger - her Soul Self during an Angel Ray Healing session with Laura Lyn.

"All of my Angel Ray Healing sessions were profoundly soothing. I felt both energized and calm. I was refreshed and a little light- headed on each of the occasions. Each was a beautiful experience and the calming effects lasted for several days after the session. But my most profound experience happened during my second session with her.

During my second visit, I was again laying on the table enjoying the lilting music and fragrant scents that filled the room. Laura had placed sacred stones at their critical points along my body and I was relaxing as her soft voice enveloped me with her love. As Laura continued calling in the angels with their Healing Rays of Light, I suddenly felt something very strange happen. I suddenly felt myself sit up. I could feel something lift out of me. My spirit-self sat up, while my physical self was still lying on the table. With my eyes still closed, I could see in my mind's eye the back, the arms, and the back of the head of this being. I felt a little startled and thought, "What's going on?" And then this being turned and looked over her left shoulder. She continued to rotate her body and left arm around and eventually turned her head around enough to look me in the eyes!

She continued to gaze softly into my eyes and then she smiled! She smiled this gentle, knowing smile, much like the Mona Lisa smile. "This is who you are!" she said to me telepathically. Her eyes were almond shaped and beautiful and expressed an unconditional love and an ancient wisdom that was strong and knowing. Her body was in the shape of a human form, but her was glowing! She glowed with a white and golden light, with hints of blue throughout. She was luminescent! She literally glowed from within! If you've ever seen the movie Cocoon, there is a scene where the young female from another star system takes off her human skin and emerges as a glowing entity. That's what I really looked like! Absolutely stunning!

She (I) possessed a wonderful combination of strength and gentleness – a perfect balance of masculine and feminine energies. She knew all, loved all and was there to be of service to others. She possessed an inner strength and quietness and assuredness that was solid and steady, and yet a softness and quietness that radiated warmth, contentment and wisdom.

As I continued to look into her eyes, I became aware of several other entities around us. They were glowing forms also, but I couldn't see their faces. It looked as though there were wearing glowing capes that made them appear soft and willowy, I hear a voice that spoke for the whole group. It said," You are one of us. You were the one from our soul group who chose to come here to Earth. We are proud of the work you are doing. We are here to assist you in any way. We are here to help you, but you must ask for assistance. We love you and want to help you on this journey." And then they all faded away.

When Laura Lyn finished the session, I explained to her what had happened. She was so excited! She said she knew something very special was happening because she could feel a strong presence in the room, way more than her usual sessions. She and I hugged each other with such happiness to have had this experience.

I am still in awe of what I saw and heard during my Angel Ray Healing sessions. I've told many people about this visionary experience because I think it's important for all of us to know two things. One, that we are all beings of Light and Love. We all glow from within and have an inner wisdom that is there for us to tap into at any time. We are balanced entities, whole and complete. We have strength from our masculine energies – and inner strength that comes from an inner knowing of Truth. And we are soft. We have a gentleness from our feminine energies that allows us to be compassionate warm and caring.

And secondly, we all need to recognize that we are not alone. We each have a soul group, a spiritual family, who watches over us and surrounds us with love and protection. This is our true family. We are the ones who are "away". They care deeply about our happiness and progress and are available to assist us. They cannot intrude and cannot assist unless asked. In the quiet time of meditation and reflection, ask your spirit family, or soul group for guidance. Ask for assistance. Ask that they show themselves to you. Your spiritual family is here with you, waiting for your requests. They'll be so thrilled to have you acknowledge them and ask for their support.

I've tried to use this experience to help me grow spiritually. I often use my imagination to visualize glowing, luminescent bodies inside each person I see. It truly changes the way you look at people. For those we see who are angry or lost, they've truly forgotten who they are. For others, there is a glimmer of understanding inside. Sometimes your eyes will meet with someone who is seeing you as a glowing spiritual being. Your eyes communicate a knowingness of who you really are. There is such joy and magic in those special moments. . . We are all glowing forms wrapped in a skin of earthly matter.

It's time for you to remember who you really are – a luminescent, spiritual being who has taken a trip to Earth to learn and grow and help others on their journey here. Wake up to the Truth of your true nature. Remember who you truly are." (25)

Information on Laura Lyn: www.angelreader.net

When Children talk to Angels

Guidance is received through ascended masters, angels, loved ones and our higher self. These experiences are happening and in such a way that our rational minds have a difficult time trying to find an explanation. Because adults tend to operate on a more rational level such experiences are often overlook or dismissed. Young children have not yet developed socialized filters, and therefore perceive the angels and loved ones from the hereafter. They don't know this isn't the norm until an adult tells them otherwise.

Stephanie, owner of a therapeutic healing business, talked with me about an experience with a Light Being when she was a little girl. Upon reflection she realized that this spiritual encounter was a message intended for her entire life. As a little girl Stephanie could see ghosts. Not realizing that others didn't see ghosts she assumed this was normal. She could see them talking, but basically just looked at them, and then returned to playing, or when visited by one during the night she went back to bed.   One evening, while staying at her grandparent's home, she was awakened.   Once again, she didn't think anything was unusual about that. Without second guessing it, she walked through the house to her grandmother's closed garage. Curious she opened the garage door. Before her stood a gigantic Being of Light- an angel. Yet at 9 years old she didn't realize this Light Being was an angel. This Light Being didn't have a face or gender. She assumed it was a woman. Yet even at a very young age, she knew that this Light Being was her higher self who was assuring her that she would always be safe. She stared at this being of Light for a very long time. They had a conversation without words, and she remembers this amazing feeling of absolute Love. She then closed the door and when back to bed.   She awakened the next day and told her mom and grandma about this experience. They laughed it off as Stephanie's imagination, so she never thought about that experience again until more recently.

As an adult, in her spiritual journey and self-reflection, Stephanie recognized that she had dismissed her own powerful experience because her mom and grandmother didn't validate it. Young children are taught to take the words of their parents, teachers and elders as the truth, even at the expense of their own experience. When people who hold such authority disregard and minimized a child's very real experience, the child will align with the adult.

The remembrance of this encounter with the Light Being reminded Stephanie that all is well and that she is profoundly loved and watched over. Additionally, she has a number that appears constantly. A combination of the number 78 confirms for her and validates choices and experiences she is meant to explore. This number offers a constant reassurance to her. Stephanie states, "Divine Guidance from the other side is so palpable if you open yourself up to it."

Divine Numerology

According to numerologists, everything in the world is dependent upon the mystical properties of numbers. These properties come from the numbers' inherent vibration. Numbers are the embodiment of vast, limitless potentials. Numeric values have been recognized throughout time for their vibrational essence, magic, symbolic, and deep spiritual meaning.

The book of Numbers is the fourth book of the Hebrew Bible, and the fourth of five books of the Jewish Torah. The book of Numbers is recorded as authored by Moses in 1450-1410 B.C. (26) Numbers mentioned in the Bible are considered to carry great spiritual meaning or symbolic significance. One can denote many meanings to these numbers according to the event or verse in the Bible.

Fibonacci numbers appear in nature revealing naturally occurring patterns. Fibonacci sequence shows that every number after the first two is the sum of the two preceding ones 1, 1, 2, 3, 5, 8, 13, 21, 34, 55, 89, 144, etc. Whether zebra's stripes, sun flowers, a spider's web, pine cones, or a snowflake, nature expresses patterns underlaid by mathematical principles.

Most numerologists credit Pythagoras with founding the field of numerology. Pythagoras was a philosopher who was born in Greece around 569 B.C. (27) Pythagoreans conclude that "all is number." Everything in this world can be measured and described in numbers and proportions. This proposition has greatly influenced science and mathematics. Another interpretation suggests that "all is number" thus meaning everything in the world originates from numbers and can be reduced to a numerical value.

Many people observe number patterns or sequences. The same number or patterns of numbers are repeated, often daily. When they look at the clock they see the same time again and again. While driving the license plate on other cars will have the same number. The repetitious occurrence of specific numbers is one way that angels and guides are communicating with you. The numbers usually hold a special personal meaning and when you see them frequently they are signs. Numbers are signs from Spirit to affirm your questions. Often when you are at a crossroad and you are seeking guidance as to what choice to make, these numbers will appear to show you that the situation you were wondering about is a Yes.

Diane L Doll, Business Consultant discusses numerology and how a specific set of numbers has guided her in many decisions. "Several years ago, I noticed that a pattern of a certain set of numbers was always included in either the phone number or address of one of the individuals or businesses that I was considering doing business with.

This set of numbers, 424, was my home address from the time I was born until age 18. Both of my parents lived there from the time they were married until they passed on.

After consulting with Angela, an Intuitive Spiritual Counselor, in February 2015, Angela explained that number 424 is a compilation of the energies and attributes of number 4 and number 2, with number 4 appearing twice, amplifying its influences. Number 4 resonates with patience, practicality and application, hard work and responsibility, traditional values, honesty and integrity, inner-wisdom, and diligence and determination to achieve goals, which were attributes of my parents also.

In addition, Number 4 relates to our drive, passion and purpose, and the energies of the Archangels. Number 2 carries the vibrations of duality, partnership and relationships, diplomacy and adaptability, sensitivity and selflessness, happiness and fulfillment. Number 2 also resonates with faith and trust and your Divine life purpose and soul mission.

Whenever faced with a decision involving a person or place to visit or do business with, or an item to purchase, route to take, etc., I look for the combination of 4's and 2's in the phone #, address, or serial number to support my choice, trusting that this combination showing up, is a message from my parents' spirit that they are helping to encourage my decisions, success, happiness and support along my path. Over the past several years, this method has never disappointed me, and it's fun to see what my spirit guides bring my way!"

Jesus Speaks

Glenda Green author of the book: Love Without End discusses the first of many visitations from Jesus. Glenda wrote, "The brilliance was intense. It filled the room so completely that all shadows departed.' 'The whole house possessed a stillness and silence of new fallen snow.' 'In the Presence there was unspeakable Holiness." (26) After the presence of light, an image of Jesus appeared to her. Jesus appeared to Glenda every day for several months. During these visits Glenda painted Jesus. The portrait of Jesus is titled 'The Lamb and the Lion. 'The story of the painting itself is a miracle. Glenda Green, an accomplished artist, her paintings are housed in major public art collections including the Smithsonian Institution. While painting Jesus, they discussed numerous topics which are revealed in her books.

Barbara Braden Kelly, Reiki Master Teacher shares a serendipitous Jesus experience revealing the message, "You are loved beyond your understanding. All is well. Most importantly, have fun."

"Twenty-seven years ago, I was experiencing fear and anxiety like I never had in my life. It was a paralyzing fear. I had been married for 16 years. Life 'had' been as close to perfect as I could have dreamed. I married my high school sweetheart at 21. We began a path of attaining the American Dream. By our 30's we had acquired it all; a successful career for my husband, financial wealth and material possessions, and a beautiful and healthy baby daughter. We had the American Dream. I can say now "The ride at Disneyland was everything we could have ever hoped for and dreamed of. Then the lights went out at Disneyland. My husband, who had his PhD, was an executive officer in his profession had what some call a 'career accident,' being in the wrong place at the wrong time.

I always say, "when you are sitting on the couch watching CNN evening news lead story and see your husband dressed in a very expensive business suit coming out of a L.A. jail in handcuffs, you know your life has 'gone to hell in a hand basket."

For the sake of my ex-husband's privacy, I will not go into the details. We are since divorced. It was a very complicated situation. It was the headlines of newspapers and the lead story on all nightly news broadcasts for weeks. He was indicted and prosecuted with many of the officers of the financial company he worked for. The trials in both federal and state took four very long years. Many of the officers went to prison. My ex-husband was eventually supported by the prosecuting attorneys by the end of the trials. He was sentenced to probation and a year of community service using his computer expertise.

I had never felt such gripping fear and an anxiety as I did for those four years. During that period, we lost almost everything we owned, the legal fees were so great. We lost our health, our wealth and the American dream. Every day I would ask "can it get worse?" and it did. My Dad/my best friend and source of unconditional love died of cancer three months prior to the indictment and beginning of the trials and my mother was diagnosed with Parkinson's and needed care.

My ex-husband spent much of those years in CA, where the state and federal trials took place. I was in our home town in the Midwest with our daughter. I was alone and afraid. It was just my young daughter and me. I worked hard to insulate and protect her from all that was going on.

There was a period in the early years of the trials where 'we' were in denial and thought once 'they' understood the structure of company they would know my ex-husband, who was described by everyone who ever met him as a 'straight arrow' and an honest person, had no part in the situation and it would end. His attorneys were not convinced this was a possibility and prepared us for the worse- case scenario. They decided with the courts. If convicted, my ex-husband would be sentenced to a minimum-security prison in a state close to where we lived so my daughter and I could visit him. It was the prison where the convicted individuals in Watergate were serving their sentences.

One day in this period, I had an especially intense day and I was trying to remain calm for my daughter's sake. I was experiencing off the scale panic and anxiety. My mind was not finding answers or peace. I could not picture the future and how I was going to handle life. I remember thinking 'I can't do this! I can't go on! I don't know how!' All I wanted to do that night was put my daughter to bed and go fall apart without her seeing me do it. She asked if I would stay with her till she fell asleep. She was seven and she understood more than I wanted her to. We laid there in her bed till she fell asleep. I was exhausted and was in that in between place where I was almost asleep and almost awake. Suddenly I felt a comfort and peace come over me. I had a flooding of warmth and a glow of happiness like I had not ever had before. 'I felt loved,' was the only way I can express it. I went from being with my daughter in her bed, to 'being' on the floor of a large domed white building. The floor was filled with people all quietly sitting facing the front where there was a stage or altar.

I felt the presence of a man sitting on my right and someone on my left. The one on my right was a man dressed in a white golf shirt and wearing navy blue pants with tiny red polka dots that were like martial arts pants. He was stroking my back very gently. I can remember looking into his face. He was very handsome, with the rugged- out- doors hiker look. He had the most loving smile and beautiful eyes that were penetrating, embracing and accepting. From him I received, not with words, but a transference of information 'You are loved beyond your understanding. All is well. Most importantly, have fun.' He just smiled at me. I remember thinking 'he looks like my cousin Michael.' I could not see the person on my left. All I could see was that it was someone with long dark hair. That fit the description of my daughter and I felt the message must have included her.

I woke up unafraid, peaceful, confident with a feeling of courage and Christmas happiness. It was a tangible feeling. I woke up feeling more loved than I had ever felt in my whole life. I had a knowing that it was all going to work out, one way or the other. If my ex-husband went to prison, my daughter and I would be fine. I also, knew I had a directive of focusing on having fun, especially with my daughter. That would be the way to get her through this period with the least impact.

The vivid memory of the experience was in my thoughts often. I kept on asking myself, "Who was this person?" I wondered if it was my guardian angel. I wondered if it was possibly Archangel Michael, since I remember thinking he looked like my cousin 'Michael.' I wondered if the person was my soulmate. For years I would look for this person in crowds hoping to find him again.

As with so many traumatic situations, couples become closer or tend go through the experience separately. Our marriage was not strong enough to endure the stress or trauma. That experience and the inner strength I came away with got me through that period. I had Inner knowing 'it was all going to work out.' I took the directive to 'have fun.' I started looking for things to do with my daughter. She and I went tent camping and adventuring. We took horseback riding and country line dancing lessons together. We bought her a dog and went through dog training classes. We became active in nature centers. We searched out ways to have fun. This was a way of life I never would have thought of without this experience. It would have been enough to just survive the experience, not have an enjoyable life going through it.

The feeling remained with me for those years of the trials and remains with me today. I can close my eyes and see the person and feel the touch of his hand on my head and back. I can still see the white shirt and the pants with tiny red polka dots that conveyed a 'most importantly, have fun' message. I still ponder that fateful night that changed my daughter's and my life forever.

Moving ahead in time, twenty- seven years later, I am divorced and happily remarried and live in TX. My daughter is grown, has her PhD and is leading a very happy and fulfilled life. Life went on and I feel had it not been for that intercession, both of our lives would have been detrimentally affected by life's circumstances.

A few years ago, a friend took me to see a portrait of Jesus that resides in a small chapel in Fort Worth. 'Ironically,' it is located on a street with the same name as my home town where I lived when I had the experience. 'Ironically,' the street before it has the same name of the county my home town city is in.

This portrait is called the 'The Lamb and The Lion.' It is painted by a very accomplished portrait artist with paintings in many museums and galleries such as the Smithsonian. She was asked to paint a portrait of Jesus. She said, "If He shows up, I would be privileged to paint him." He did. She has a fascinating story and book of this experience.

When my friend and I drove up I had the calmness and happiness I had the night I had my experience. We walked in and sat down, we became very quiet and I had a 'knowing' this was the time for me to realize 'who' that person was that sat down next to me that night. The handsome man with the loving eyes and smile that gave me my lifeline to get through those years was, indeed, the man in this painting. There are many paintings and people's ideas of what Jesus looked like. The man that sat next to me 'was' the man in this painting, not that he looked like the portrait. I had, and sometimes still do have, a hard time justifying and accepting it.

I have asked many times "Who am I to have had a direct experience of Jesus?" To that I hear the response "Who are you to not have a direct experience?"

I grew up Methodist and my family went to the church at the end of our street as a community social activity. I went to a Religious Society of Friends/Quaker college in my hometown because I could live at home and go to college. I was required to take many hours of religion classes to graduate and required to attend several mandatory weekly chapels. The chapel time would be with a ministerial teaching and people would come forward to give testimonies. I was not comfortable in this setting. I gave up on religiosity, Christianity, and 'churchianity.'

I thought of Jesus as an interesting person in the history of religion. I 'threw out the baby with bath water.' I set out as a seeker/searcher for most of my life in Buddhism, Hinduism, Taoism, Native American Spirituality, New Age and Metaphysical studies. Finding myself giving this 'testimony' makes me realize how full circle my life has come.

In this past year, with the acceptance of this personal relationship with Jesus, I have become a student of the teachings of Parmahansa Yogananda, author of 'Autobiography of a Yogi,' who came to the US from the India in the early 1920's to unite the ancient philosophy of Kriya Yoga and the teachings of Christianity. I now have an understanding that the person sitting on my left the night I experienced Jesus was indeed, Guruji Yogananda.

I am so happy that Daria asked me to contribute to her book. I have only relayed the story of that life altering night with a few people over the years. I have not been comfortable recounting the experience to many others. It feels too like those mandatory chapel testimonies.

Writing it and recounting it now feels like part of the plan. "Who am I to have a direct experience of the One who loves me the most?" "Who am I not to have this experience?" I ask you to ask yourself this same question and listen for the answer. Do not wait until you are paralyzed with fear. Do it now, do it frequently."

Spirit Animal Guides

Often when we take a walk in the woods, or an evening walk around our own back yard we discover a feather. Consider that the hawk, owl, or even the sweet white dove feather is a gift and message from Spirit. Notice the timing of receiving such treasures. These little gifts are often ways, loved ones and Spirit guides communicate with us. Other times we are the recipients of direct communication with animals from both the physical realms and spiritual realms.

In the early spring of 2000, I moved to a country home. One morning I awoke to a loud noise of a hawk screeching outside my window. I was tired from a long work week, so I ignored the hawk the best I could by putting a pillow over my head, so I could sleep a little longer. The hawk persisted so reluctantly I got up. I remember reading somewhere that hawks are messengers. I walked outside, and the hawk looked into my eyes and I asked him if he had a message for me. I received an impression of a man I knew named Wolf Eyes, so feeling a little foolish I ask the hawk if the message was this man. The moment I asked that question the Hawk flew away. The answer was yes. Life connected us within a couple of days. The result of this connection then led me to taking a trip with a group of Lakota Indians to a traditional Sundance near Mobridge, SD. Mobridge is one hour from Standing Rock Indian Reservation ND. There I participated in the Sundance. I learned amazing traditions of the Lakota (Sioux) people. To write about all that I learned with the Lakota and specifically through Wolf Eyes, Alvera Pipebear the powerful Medicine woman, and David my Lakota brother would take the space of an entire book. The experiences and things I participated in and witnessed irrevocably change me in a powerful way.

Spirit is talking to us all the time with perfect guidance for our life's journey. All we need to do is stop and listen. Often the most obvious solution or idea is right in front of us. We don't see it because we are busy doing so many other things and we miss the divine answer to our questions. There was a time when humanity recognized itself as part of nature. We had an instinctive tie to all of creation. We never lost our connectedness to all of life, because Oneness can't be divided. What we lost is our awareness of our connectedness to all life. Just as there are many facets that make up our being beyond the physical there are many facets and relationships with animals.

The hawks have communicated and continue to do so year after year. When I hear the Hawk's cry, I am moved with deep emotion. Hawks have the power to soar high above the earth giving them a perspective previously only available to the inhabitants of the heavens above. Because of this people from various cultures throughout history regard the hawks as messengers of spirit bringing wisdom from the heavens. From their vantage point riding on the wind and sunlight they remind us that there is a bigger picture than our current realities presentation. They remind us that we are part of a larger plan and that everything fits together beautifully and perfectly. Hawks were thought to be able to look directly into the sun and see what is not visible to the rest of us. By looking within, ourselves we find our own inner light that guides us, allowing us to see clearly what is not visible unless actively sought.

David my Lakota brother Sun dancer had an animal totem that was the dragonfly. Therefore, whenever David was around dragonflies were around. The third year David danced I did not make the journey to South Dakota. I told David when he needed my support to just call on me energetically and I would be there sending distance healing, prayers and support. That year I was in New York at Lilly Dale. I was sitting with a crowd of people at a place called inspiration stump. Suddenly a swarm of dragonflies showed up only in the row I was sitting in. The women sitting next to me were trying to fling them away because there where so many. I said Oh that's David needing prayer and support. Immediately the dragonflies left. I silently sent my prayers and support. It was confirmed later that at that very same time that day, David was indeed needing my prayers and energetic support.

The dragonfly represents new perspectives of making a change in one's own life. I have had a dragonfly land on my hand for over an hour. The same experience occurred with a butterfly. Both times where times of me facing changes in my life.

Wolf medicine entered my life with a vengeance via a relationship. Wolf is regarded as one of the most powerful spirit guides of all, and its presence is a message of guidance and knowledge. It wasn't until years later when I took a two- month sabbatical at a cabin in the forest by the Canadian border that Wolf came as a personal guardian.

I was searching in earnest for relief from suffering. I was seeking for answers to help me relate to my own feelings of grief, shock, and despair. I was seeking relief from the pain of a broken heart and shattered dreams. It had been only a few months since my son died and I couldn't stand to be around people, so I went to live in a cabin on my cousin's property in Hovland, MN. The cabin was surrounded by a forest of Mid November trees. Stripped naked of their canopy, white birch and aspen stood tall revealing spontaneous yet quiet displays of autumn sunrises. This "hunters" cabin fueled by a wood burner, no electric, no running water is nestled in the middle of a forest. I'm told there are one paved road, one railroad track, and half dozen dirt roads between here and the Arctic Circle.

My mind failed to mentally grasp this prodigious area. Never have I lived off the grid, so there was no frame of reference to recognize this place for what it was. My mind interpreted this wilderness as a wooded park surrounded by community. Such is the nature of the mind. The mind relegates the present moment to past experiences and uses the criteria for perception. We view our world through the lens of our past.

Nearly a full moon rose as a spot light through the winter forest. The sun had set twenty minutes' prior. The time was 4:25 pm and it has been three weeks there at the cabin. I kept a journal. As I put pen to paper next to a lantern, the warmth of the wood burner warmed my body, but not deeply enough. There was a penetrating cold inside. Only the re-emergence of personal life force would fuel the life force that was like the red glow of coals the morning after a camp fire. At least there were a few sparks emerging out of the ash. Candle light helped me see the pages to write. The average temperature was a glorious 19 degrees with partial sunny skies. Earlier that day I hiked following the deer trails along the ridge toward the north shore of Lake Superior. Looking for tracks I found deer and tracks of a canine nature. A few nights ago, I heard the wolf pack howl. Then later that night when I stepped outside the cabin I made eye contact with a wolf's eyes from within the trees. Quickly I retreated inside. The cabin sits in the middle of a forest seven miles south of the Canada border. This was wolf country.

The following day I sat still in silence and noticed as thoughts and emotions emerged. As they calmed, a deep penetrating sadness began to re-emerge. The same sadness that surfaces in the middle of the night as I look up at the northern display of star filled sky. The same sadness that sat in the middle of my throat when I talked to my daughter trying to find the balance between being authentic and having a supportive positive conversation with her. The same sadness when I put on a happy face as I interacted with a small group of people. A couple of months prior to my stay at my cousin's cabin, I noticed several people commented that I was "doing really well" handling the grief from the loss of my son. The truth was I was in emotional shock. I presented a pulled together persona. But that was merely a surface façade. They didn't look deeper. Regardless there is a level of communication that occurs beyond verbal interactions.

Interestingly on this day, as my mind cleared through meditation, I felt and saw the image of a wolf in my mind. This was the same type of image one has when they see a face of a loved one and they receive a phone call in the next moments from that same person. The wolf that I had made eye contact with the previous day was checking me out. I was silent enough in my mind to notice and connect back. The wolf connection felt penetrating and strong. Reflecting on this, I realize that the connection was a pivotal moment for me to stand strong against all odds. It was a strength I would need come December of that year to stand in my power making a choice regardless of how beaten down I was.

My cousin Mark who lives there in MN shared that during hunting season the deer leave the fields to hide in the trees. The next day after hunting season is over the deer go back out to the fields. They sense and know the hunter's thoughts. There is a whole world of knowing and absolute clear awareness that is available to every human. Clear your thoughts first to experience this revelation. Animals already have it. We used to have this knowing before the modern age of so many distractions.

Spirit guides reveal themselves as animals either in dreams, or meditations and through physical animals. These powerful Beings are protectors and magnificent Spiritual teachers and guides. Sit down in meditation or take a walk in the woods and ask for your guide at this time to be revealed to you.

My Life long Spirit Animal guide is the Deer. In the summer of 2008 I spent a week in silence at River's Edge Monastery. When you quiet your voice, it doesn't take long to realize just how noisy one's mind is. After a few days of working on quieting my mind, I took a walk through the woods feeling quite loud in my head. I sensed something watching me, so I looked in that direction and saw a beautiful large buck watching me. He wasn't just pretending to be frozen like deer do when they encounter humans. This was different. His gaze penetrated my mind and heart, and from that moment forward my mind became quiet and peaceful. The rest of the week I walked with the deer. St Francis would be so proud!

Spirit is always teaching and communicating with us, whether through angels, ascended masters, people, animals, a song on the radio, something you read, or a feeling inside. All one needs to do is listen.

Know that your sincere prayers are answered according to Divine Will. Divine intervention is a common occurrence. Consider all that must come into play just for us to be alive. That in itself is a miracle. Heavenly light beings are watching over you. They communicate to you in dreams and sometimes premonitions. Inspired ideas generate new growth and opportunities. The Aha moments, flashes of insight connect the puzzle pieces and become the catalyst for change. When change arrives don't resist or hold back. Take a deep breath in, exhaling step out of the boat onto faith.

The Divine Mother

The Divine Mother is called by many names such as Goddess, Mother Mary, Durga, Tara, Quan yin, and Europa. The forms of the Goddess are countless, but there is only one Divine Mother or Sacred Feminine behind them all. Ultimately the Mother is pure formless Love appearing as the manifold expressions we see as the universe and all the beings in nature. By acknowledging the Mother in any of Her forms, we will eventually arrive at the non-dual perspective.

The Neolithic settlement of Catal Huyuk (c.7000 BC) in Anatolia provides archaeological evidence that the worship of the Divine Mother Goddess experienced a long continuity. Numerous texts discuss the Divine Mother influential role in all cultures. In these earlier mythologies, the Mother was that which gives birth to all creatures and that the earth, the elements, were not void of spirit but are in fact the living Goddess-Creator herself.

The concept of a feminine God is not new. Virtually every culture has worshiped a Supreme Being in a female form. For example, Hindu and Buddhist cultures are rife with forms of the Divine Mother such as Tara and Durga. The study of early Gnostic Christians reveals the Virgin Sophia who is the feminine embodiment of Wisdom. The Chinese have Kwan Yin the Goddess of Mercy. In orthodox Judaism, there is the Sabbath Queen and the feminine Shekinah. Mother Mary, the virgin mother of Jesus, continues the presence of the Divine Mother in modern Christianity.

In embarking on a brief study with Guru Leela Mata at Peaceful Valley Ashram, I learned about another aspect of the Divine Mother.

Durga (meaning invincible one) is the principal form of the Mother Goddess in Hinduism. She is known by a variety of names - including Amba,

Ambika, Jagadamba, Parvathi, Shakti, Adishakti, Adi Parashakti and Devi. Durga is regarded by Hindus as the root cause of creation, sustenance and annihilation. She is pure energy (referred to as "Shakti" in Sanskrit and Hindu religious context). Being innately formless, she manifests herself within the gods so that she may fulfill the tasks of the universe via them. At times of distress, she manifests herself in divine form to protect the world.

Durga is the supreme soul, otherwise called Shakti (primordial cosmic energy). She is the original cause of all the past, present and future worldly occurrences.

Whatever her name Durga, Parvati or Mother Mary, this Divine Being is considered the Pure Form of Light that exists prior to and within all of creation. Many cultures consider a visit from the Divine Mother the highest possible blessing and healing one can receive. As a healer, working with powerful healing vibrations such as Reiki, ascended masters, angels, light beings, crossed over loved ones, and the many forms of God and Goddesses will come to assist in the healing sessions. Lisa Rockwell, Intuitive Energy Healer describes one such encounter with Mother Mary.

"While volunteering Reiki at a local cancer center, I witnessed many miraculous healings and blessings. Reiki is a Japanese healing modality for stress reduction and relaxation, it is also divine energy that welcomes benevolent beings to step forth to provide the healings. One of my most memorable Reiki sessions is when I looked up and saw Mother Mary touching the person on the table. Carol was having sinus and chest pain with trouble breathing. She was worried that it might be her heart again. She already had a heart attack and knew the symptoms all too well. Insisting that her pains were not alarming enough to go to the doctor, she jumped up on the Reiki table with anticipation of what I would find was wrong with her. I reminded her that I never know what the outcome of the healing session would be and that I was just the open vessel for God's energies to flow through. Carol also knew that I received visions and could see energetic imbalances within the body.

Many messages from Spirit and those that had passed on from this Earth plane were also occurring with every session. She smiled and said, "I am ready."

The session began with a Prayer of Gratitude to God for the healing energy that flows into me and out of my hands. I placed my hands upon her head where I connected with her essence. The divine energy began to flow, and Carol quickly fell asleep. She was breathing at a relaxed pace throughout the entire session. As I altered the energies throughout her body, she became more relaxed. Stagnant energy was being released while radiant divine energy flowed into her.

I was in awe as I watched Mother Mary stand before me. She was wearing a veil over a long dress that flowed down her back and covered the sides of her body. She dissolved right before my eyes leaving her glow and the gentlest energy that held intense unconditional love.

I could not wait until the session was over to hear her experience. Carol woke up and I asked her how she felt. She responded, "I am good." I asked how her chest was. Her eyes got bigger with her surprise that her chest felt good. After sharing with her what happened, she was feeling blessed and said, "I hope that it lasts." I told her that it will last, however; she needs to believe that a healing had occurred physically, emotionally or on a mental level. When one disbelieves that they are not healed, then discomfort and illness may return.

Jesus has also been appearing with Mother Mary during the sessions. There are many ways that they assist in the healings, observing, laying their hands upon the body or one of them will walk into my body to assist with the healing. Miraculous blessings surround all of us, all that you need to do is to ask and you shall receive."

Water cuts through rock not
because of its power, but
because of its Persistence.

Chapter 6

Twenty-one Days

Change is knocking on your door. It's time to go within and seek the guidance of your own intuition. We no longer have the luxury to postpone the inner work that needs to be done. It's time to stop running around and worrying about the future. Release your grievances, all of them. Consider that the words on this page are a message from your Spirit guides and your higher self. Are you listening? To get to where you want to be which is not where you are currently at, a life map is provided for you. To access this map, allow everything to fall away except the stillness of the moment. In sitting in silence and aligning with the

Divine you will be lead to the highest outcome for your life journey. In a single still moment of surrender miracles are born. No longer can you look for answers outside. The true power lies reflected in the still waters within you.

Get real with yourself, by examining your patterns. Are you doing the same thing over and over thinking, "This time it will be different, and I have control over this?" Release that thinking. Surrender your life and everything you struggle with to the Divine so that something new and in alignment with your true nature can emerge.

Sometimes when you have done all you can, giving 100% effort into a new practice the results of those efforts are minimal if at all. Take heart in knowing that the integration and anchoring happens in the pause.

As a massage therapist I have worked on over 13,000 clients. The muscles integrate and relax in the pause between the physical massaging. This is how the nervous system is designed. This is also reflected in life. There is a rhythm and a season for everything. When you align with the natural rhythms of life your experiences will be full of grace and ease. When you take sabbaticals for yourself, preferably daily, the positive transformation will be astounding. For most people this takes consistent effort with repetition. Except for extreme traumatic events, a person didn't develop lack and limitation vibrations overnight. This was and is a gradual process of entrainment from the influences of the outer world.

Often a person will seek and explore self -help genre because of disappointment and disillusionment in their life. Sometimes we don't get what we want, or a situation fails to work out because there is something better in store. Sometimes when you feel like you are going nowhere it is because you are meant to stay put.

In 2012, I moved out West with a new husband. I had a dream to live there since I was 18 years old. One month after the move my son died. I came home to bury my son and to grieve. Five months after my son died my husband asked for a divorce. Because of the divorce I never made it back to live in the West. Other minor events collaborated to keep me in my home town. I wasn't happy about any of it. Today, 6 years later, I still live in my home town. I have the profound joy of babysitting my 2-year-old granddaughter during the week. I completed my post graduate studies and have a PhD in Philosophy. Since 2012, I have authors 24 books. Had I move back West, I would have missed these precious years with my granddaughter. If I was still married, I know I would never have gone back to school or written as many books.

When experiencing hard times, have courage and dare to dream no matter what the circumstances. Not only will you survive, you will thrive. It is during dry spells that we discover our true inner power, courage and faith. Every life has a desert period. If you are feeling parched from you own long desert walk, sit down in the shade. Connect with and intend a nourishing divine energy flowing into your entire being. Fill yourself up from within. Make this a daily practice and over time your oasis will emerge. Through daily practice a habit is formed. When the habit is formed you will look forward to your daily communion.

Have you ever thought of picking up a good habit, but never got around to doing it? Perhaps you tried to do so for one-two days yet lacked the discipline to continue. It seems that the moment you decided to start a spiritual practice your children or spouse, work etc., increased their demands on your attention. Maybe you feel exhausted and this would be one more thing to add to your already overloaded to do list. Perhaps you are overwhelmed by the effort needed to develop the new habit. Your mind will give you numerous reasons to delay a new practice. Stop procrastinating. The journey of a thousand miles begins with a single step.

The mind contracts back with discouraging thoughts when the goal is overwhelming. That is why once the vision is in place, smaller manageable steps are necessary to actuate results. Adopt a mindset of "just for today". The one day at a time philosophy is associated with 12 step groups such as Alcoholics Anonymous. Dara Drug and Alcohol Rehab in Thailand states; "The Just for Today Card is often read out at 12 step meetings. It includes several commitments that people pledge themselves to stick to over the next 24 hours. It includes the intention to:

* Live through just one day and not try to deal with all of life's problems at once.

* Commit to being happy for the next 24 hours.

* Promise to learn new things and strengthen the mind.

* Commit to do things for other people and act in an agreeable manner

* Follow a recovery program with as much effort as possible

* Commit to take at least 30 minutes for relaxation and quite reflection

* The promise to enjoy life and not be afraid of things

> The center's philosophy declares; "It is only possible to find happiness in this moment. The song _Beautiful Boy, Darling Boy by John Lennon says, life is what happens to you while you're busy making other plans. Too many people spend their time focused on the future, and this means that they miss all the joy that is available right now. Being

caught in the future becomes a habit that leads to a great deal of dissatisfaction with life. Living one day at a time does not mean that people should ignore the future. They should still plan for their retirement and keep money aside for a rainy day. The advice is that people should avoid being too focused on the future, particularly about things that are unknowable." (9)

Some people will feel they do not have 30 minutes for relaxation and quiet reflection. If you don't have 30 minutes to pause, start by committing to five or ten minutes of silence and simply Be with yourself.   To affect the desired shifts that your heart and soul are longing for this practice needs to be done daily. I have put together a 21-day process that will guide you and illuminate the spaces and places crying out for healing.

Why 21 days? Celestine Chua, founder of Personal Excellence Co in her article developing a good habit in 21 days states; "According to research, it takes 21 days to fully form a new habit, as 21 days is the time required for new neuropathways to be fully formed in your brain. Brain circuits take engrams (memory traces) and produce neuro-connections and neuropathways only if they are bombarded for 21 days in a row. This means that our brain does not accept new data for a change of habit unless it is repeated each day for 21 days (without missing a day)." (10)

> Dr. Mercola in her article on Neuroplasticity states; "As time goes by, science provides more and more evidence that your brain is malleable and continually changing in response to your lifestyle, physiology, and environment. This concept is called neuroplasticity, or brain plasticity—meaning, you are literally reforming your brain with each passing day. It used to be thought that your brain was

static, except during some critical developmental periods, but today, we know this isn't true. Your brain possesses the remarkable ability to reorganize pathways, create new connections and, in some cases, even create new neurons throughout your entire lifetime." (11)

Create a place of refuge, a place where you can go to sit and simply be. This doesn't have to be an elaborate set up. It is more important to cultivate a consistent practice daily where you go to the same place. A simple chair in the corner of a room is enough. To help draw the focus to a daily practice many people find it beneficial to create an altar adored with cherish or inspired objects. Anything that evokes a positive feeling such as flowers, a photo of an ascended master, candles or crystals is recommended. I have a blanket that holds the blessings from a Sundance tree. When I use the blanket as a shawl and wrap it around me a conditioned response is immediately evoked where my mind settles. Let the space you create beckon you to sit in stillness and simply be present whenever the need arises.

Begin your practice by setting a daily intention. My primary daily intention is to connect with Divinity to align as a vibrational expression of Love. From this alignment I ask for guidance and direction. I make the statement, "I now decide to be fully all that I already am, and I now live from this space. I embody the highest vibrational outcome needed this day."

Every day is an opportunity. Every day you can start fresh and plant a seed that your consciousness will nourish to fruition. Utilize the power of intention to shine the light of your consciousness on what it is you want to achieve. Your intention might be to soften your reactions or choose to be grateful in each moment, it could be ongoing or short term. Whatever it is, let your intention guide you to alignment with the energy you wish to embody.

Day 1

Change around the corner

Is there divisiveness in any of your relationships either professional or personal? Do you find that you are out of sync with another or your life in general? Do the once comfortable dynamics of your life no longer feel right? As much as you try to re-create past positive moments you can't, because life doesn't tarry with yesterday. Life is expansive thus moves forward reaching for a future. The evolution of you reveals unequivocal inner changes. As a result, people that once held the spotlight start to drift away. As you change, your personal vibration changes. This means you begin to broadcast a different frequency which attracts new matching relationships and opportunities.

When you are embarking on transformation the Universe/Providence will give you signs. We are not meant to navigate life journeys along. During pivotal times in life it is important to pause and connect in with Source/God. In fact, the busier life is the more important it is to take those moments of pause. Meditate or pray and listen for the inner guidance that can be heard in stillness and silence.

When you are not seeing the signs or listening to the promptings of your heart your sleep patterns may change. Are you more tired than usual? Is it increasingly more difficult to wake up?

Some changes in the sleep patterns can cue you into changes happening in your heart and mind. You may also find yourself wanting to sleep more often, or even find it harder to wake up. Do you awaken at the same time in the middle of the night, then toss and turn? Often this is the result of your brain attempting to reconcile the parts of your life that are out of alignment with your true desires. As your path becomes clear to you, and past unresolved traumas are integrated, your sleep patterns will most likely normalize. Both resolving past traumas and listening to the guidance of your soul directing your future require your presence. Most people are so immersed in busy daily schedules that their inner guidance can only communicate with them in the middle of the night.

If you have grown out of the last phase of your life, previous ways of relating and approaching situations usually won't grant the same results. Additionally, another indicator that change is around the corner is the urge to resolve old issues, tie up loose ends in business, and have that heart to heart conversation. During a transformational time, you may discover that your emotions and feelings wield strongly. Your emotions are powerful indicators and will teach you about yourself.

Sit still for a moment. Watch your thoughts the way you watch a movie. Feel into your emotions. What do they reveal? Your mind has an astounding way of rationalizing. Your emotions and body communicate how you truly feel about a situation or circumstance. Acknowledge how you feel without judgement or trying to change anything. Then ask Providence; "What is your vision for me and my life"? Be patient for you to discern and know the answer.

Day 2

Paradoxical Intent

The University of Illinois describes the eye of a storm; "Skies are often clear above the eye and winds are relatively light. It is the calmest section of any hurricane. The eye is so calm because the now strong surface winds that converge towards the center never reach it. The coriolis force deflects the wind slightly away from the center, causing the wind to rotate around the center of the hurricane (the eye wall), leaving the exact center (the eye) calm." (9) Annemarie Schneider the artist of the book cover for Walk on Water states: "We all have our own storms within where we have to fight to calm it. You can see it in someone's eyes, sometimes when all they need or want is a safe place to feel love and peace." (10)

The Law of Paradoxical Intent is defined as operating in alignment with and harnessing the power of the universal principle, "What you resist persists." (11) By using the power of your will and intention to increase the symptom you have been automatically trying to decrease, resistance disappears, and therefore, persistence disappears. Life is a constant barrage of moment to moment experiences. Instead of flowing with life most people grasp and seek to hold on to experiences they like and resist the ones they don't. Both grasping and resisting energetically forestalls new future experiences. One remains stuck in a conceptual world which only dwells in the past.

Today pause and notice your thoughts in relationship to events and people around you. Are there places where you are resisting? Resistance feels contracted and stuck.

Just notice. Become aware. When feeling in a contracted state, take a moment and pause. With intention, expand your energy from your heart out in a circle. Visualize a warm golden glow creating circles of love energy around your heart, then expanding around your body, and then seven more rings around each other until the entire room is filled. Expand further if you want around the building, the city block, the state, country, world, or universe. Next, focus inward on your heart. Breathe in deeply and exhale a few times. Bring the Love that you are in to your heart space. Surround the part of you that is feeling unloved or struggling with worry etc. with this spacious infinite love. Affirm by saying, "I Love You". "I approve of you." Self- approval makes you pre-approved for every encounter in your life. When you embody self-love and approval, you become free from another's manipulation and control. When you fully accept and embrace you the world can simply be as it is. Then you become an embodiment light that shifts everything simply by being your natural state which is Love.

Day 3

In the gap

When you take off the rose- colored glasses the polarity of life reveals the darker tragic side. But take comfort in the truth that loss and the collateral emotions of pain, grief, anger and self-doubt are just a few threads in the tapestry of life. It is the nature of the mind to react negatively to tragic life experiences. The mind dictates every life experience by the narratives that it tells itself. When our thoughts believe 'this isn't how life was supposed to be,' we set ourselves at odds with life. Life just is the way it is. Our judgments and opinions construct our reality. It is imperative to become conscious and aware of the mental constructs that create the experience of suffering and sorrow. Sorrow is not caused by life, but by the opinions and judgments one has made in relation to challenging life experiences. What is your basic emotional orientation toward life? Have you ever considered that question? Interpretations and declarations on how life should be are narratives that have no fundamental basis. The narratives of the mind emerge because we have separated ourselves from life. The separation was created in the mind because we judge. Because you know you judge, you have the freewill to choose to embrace challenges with loving kindness or be at odds with it. Life is happening, and your mind is narrating a story about it. Then you live a story. You are not your mind. If you were you wouldn't know that you have thoughts. Who you are is so much more. Learn to live in the gap between the mind's stories. When thoughts are active the brain looks like a lightning storm. Stand in the eye of the storm.

Here you will know that harmonizing with life is far easier than living in opposition to it.

What does it feel like when you are "in the gap" between thoughts? Have you ever been there? Begin a meditation practice. Even for a few minutes, pause, and be still. Breathe in, pause, Breathe out. Pay attention to the pause in between breaths. Linger there.

Day 4

Practicing Acceptance

Even stresses and problems will pass as all things are impermanent. How soon or how long depends on you and you alone. Problems, and stressors can be an invitation for you to reconnect with the aspects of yourself that wish to be liberated. Therefore, they serve a purpose in the realization of oneness. Everyone experiences emotions of sadness, anger, fear, and self-doubt. These feelings and emotions are not exclusive to you. The 1st step towards peace and freedom is to accept all emotions within yourself. To the degree that you accept all of you is equal to your acceptance of others in the world around you. Through acceptance a clarity emerges allowing you a broader perspective and the ability to see the greater Universal truths.

Alcoholics Anonymous Big Book quotes–
"Acceptance is the answer to ALL of my problems
today. When I am disturbed, it is because I find
some person, place, thing or situation- some fact of
my life- unacceptable to me, and I can find no
serenity until I accept that person, place, thing, or
situation as being exactly the way it is supposed to
be at this moment. Nothing, absolutely nothing,
happens in God's world by mistake." (12)
Acceptance is an ongoing practice. For each
moment that an emotion arises that you'd rather
not face and experience, you're given an
opportunity to compassionately and
unconditionally love you including every disturb
thought and every dark emotion. Choosing
acceptance doesn't mean you have to agree with or
even like what you are in acceptance of. Rather you
are aligning with whatever is in any given
moment. When you choose to accept things as
they are, you free up all the energy you've been

using to resist life. The heart and soul accept things completely as they are.

Today, notice if you are in non-acceptance in relation to anything or anyone. If you are experiencing opposition then accept your non-acceptance. Then explore acceptance. Does your body relax when you are in acceptance? Is it tense when you are not?

Day 5

Give up Control

When life has prompted changes, people often fall back into old behaviors and make choices that never worked before, but they think that this time it will be different. "It" will only be different when you choose to approach life in a different way. When you hit bottom embrace the change and surrender control. As difficult as it is to accept, and you have reached a point where you can go no further in the same manner, let go of your grip. Consciously release the desire for control.

There are many debates regarding free will. You have free will which means you have the power to act of your own accord or your own volition. Yet You cannot control how or in the way life is unfolding for you. Control is an illusion. Because it is illusionary, control is another form of resistance. Control is the action born out of your conditioning and lack of trust. The act of control inhibits your ability to flow with the rhythm of life. Control removes you from being present in each moment.

It is not your responsibility to control what the Universe is outwardly manifesting in any given moment. You are only accountable and responsible for your personal vibrational energy signature. Your only job is to remain conscious as you continuously strive to deepen your connection to God/Source. Give up control and enjoy the new simplicity and freedom. Providence has a vision for your life that eclipses anything you could imagine. Give up control by practicing acceptance.

If acceptance challenges you, know that you're not alone. Acceptance requires practice. The act of conscious acceptance allows you to release all the heavy thoughts and emotions that weigh you down.

There's a profound power in letting go of control. By letting go how you relate to the world shifts from your ego mind to your heart. You move from judge to witness; from wanting to manifesting. You were never meant to carry so many heavy burdens. Recognize that nothing needs to be any different, and everything can just be what it is in every moment. No part of you or another, and no part of your past needs to be fixed or changed, rather it just needs to be seen through the eyes of love and acceptance. If you are not in acceptance you are in resistance which is control. When you stop resisting life, life will stop resisting you. When we stop judging our life we become unlimited and completely free. Declare yourself free and live it. Give over life to God/Source. When we stop judging our life peace becomes our companion. Release control and experience the peace that only surrender can deliver.

Take a personal inventory of all the places and spaces you feel the need to control. Most of us have a list, therefore; you may want to write this down. Notice the dialogue your mind holds. Now focus your awareness on your heart. Look within as you place your hands over your heart. Ask the question, "What would love do"?

Day 6

Inner Connection

You may feel mentally scattered and be struggling to communicate your thoughts to others. Social events may make you feel overwhelmed and intimidated, and even smaller gatherings could contribute to feelings of oversensitivity. By first understanding that your mental confusion could be caused by a feeling of disconnection from your inner self, you will realize that you can remedy this situation by spending some quality time alone. As you remove yourself from external distractions, release overwhelming thoughts, and turn your attention inward, you should feel a greater sense of clarity and balance return to your mind, body, and spirit.

By fostering a strong connection with our inner selves, we benefit from a heightened sense of clarity and balance in all areas of our lives. Disconnection from our spiritual center often causes us to feel scattered and out of touch with even important aspects of our lives. Getting reconnected is a simple matter of removing distractions and turning our attention inward to focus on the integration of our body, mind, and spirit. This helps us open our awareness and tune in to the spiritual wisdom within us, which can help us feel more balanced and connected in our lives. With inner balance and stronger clarity, we feel less overwhelmed and ready to participate joyfully in life again. If you focus on strengthening your connection from the inside out today, you will be able to release your scattered feelings and connect with others in meaningful ways again.

Pause for a moment. Take a deep breath in. As you exhale relax your shoulders. Draw your attention to your feet. Feel the surface under you touching your feet. What does the floor feel like under your feet? Is the carpet soft, or firm, warm or cool? Do you have shoes on? If so, become aware of both how the shoes feel on your feet and how the surface of the earth feels under you. Simply notice the contact point between your feet and the surface under them. As you walk around today be mindful of the ground under your feet. Walk on the concrete, then walk on the grass. Notice that there is a difference in sensation. Notice the difference of when you walk in the city verses walk in the woods. Specifically keep your focus to a singular point of your feet in relationship to the earth. Once a connection is established with the earth, you are drawing away from the mental chatter of your mind an into the seat of the self.

Day 7

Think about it

Did you know that every thought you think is non-verbal communication? All verbal and non-verbal communications transmit energy. The thoughts we have about other people have the same level of energy vibration as if they are spoken aloud. All thoughts and scenarios that we create through our imagination are experienced energetically. Contemplate an interaction you had with another. Even though they may have been professional and polite, the interaction felt heavy. You may have felt great, then after the interaction you walked away feeling drained or foggy in your thinking. It is very likely that they were holding negative non-supportive thoughts. Now think about an interaction with another, someone you feel safe and comfortable around no matter what. Notice how uplifted you feel after talking with them. Their thoughts and feelings toward you are congruent with their outer verbal dialogue. The message here is to become mindful of your thinking. Are you in acceptance or non-acceptance? You will know by the feeling of contraction or expansion. You have only one task in this life that is yours alone to accomplish and that is being aware and responsible for the energy you bring to every moment.

Are you in judgment and resistance or in complete acceptance? Practice giving up your personal opinions regarding everything. This won't be easy especially with certain situations and people who are triggers. After a life time of your mind offering judgements on everything, halting the process will take consistent practice. If you master this, you will be the embodiment of Pure Awareness and Pure Unconditional Love. You will walk on water!

As you move through your day, pay attention to your inner dialogue. Notice that your mind has an opinion about everything. Notice the judgements and lovingly relax and breathe. Notice thought patterns and release. Again, notice thought patterns and release. Do not judge your judgments. Lovingly accept that this is what you do, because your mind is trying to protect you. Simply notice, then choose to let go.

Day 8

What isn't Broken

We've been conditioned from the earliest years of our lives to believe that we are broken, that we are deficient and that in some way, someone or something outside of us has an answer or solution to all our issues in life. This false conditioning has been handed down from generation to generation. After all, society can only teach what they know. All beliefs are deeply rooted through cultural influence. Culture is, in the words of E.B. Tylor, "that complex whole which includes knowledge, belief, art, morals, law, custom and any other capabilities and habits acquired by man as a member of society."(13) Certain religions monopolize on the premises that to be human is to be flawed, incomplete, and with sin. For example, the Bible Psalm 51:5 states; "Surely I was sinful at birth, sinful from the time my mother conceived me." (14)

It is imperative that you erase the belief of brokenness or sinfulness because as you believe this you can never fully actualize and realize all that you are. The authentic you will continue to remain elusive in the background. Because of this conditioning that has spanned generations, people are constantly trying to fix something about themselves that doesn't need to be fixed. When you focus on what you perceive to be the flawed aspect of yourself that viewpoint energetically locks the wrongness in place. If you dwell on the clouds the sun will forever remain concealed.

As a medical massage therapist, I was trained to identify structural problems and taught the treatments to remedy the condition. Over the years working with 13,000 plus clients I notice that the muscles relaxed quicker and easier when I relaxed my own body and communicated through touch the experience of ease, movement, and relaxation. When I stopped trying to change the client's muscles from painful tight to relaxed and communicated peaceful acceptance the results were immediate and astounding. Only real unconditional love can liberate you through integration. This Love is your authentic expression. It moves you into connection with the Universal fabric of existence.

Today practice holding every part of you in unconditional love. Call forth your darkest guilt and lovingly imagine holding this in the same way a mother comforts her baby.

Healing Visualization to break free of Broken

Find a safe quiet place where you won't be disturbed. Silence your cell phone. Bring a glass of water with you. Sit in a comfortable position and relax your shoulders. Become aware of your breath. Slow down your breathing by taking a few deep long breaths. If you feel thirsty take a few sips of water, then return to your breath. As you begin to relax notice your feet. Become aware of the space of contact between your feet and the surface under. With intention visualize connecting with the earth. Like the cord from a cell phone plugs into the outlet to recharge, plug into the earth through your feet. Know that you are completely supported. Draw your intention upward to God/Divine Source. Visualize the holy light or holy spirit flowing into and around you. You are fully supported and loved. Now welcome all energies from beliefs that hold you trapped in this belief of brokenness. Ask for all thoughts, feelings and emotions that perpetuate the experience of unlovable, and unworthy to come forward. Ask for that which holds you apart from complete personal empowerment to be revealed to your awareness. Perhaps a parent or someone who was in a position of authority spoke their false beliefs over you when you were a child. What is true for another doesn't need to be true for you unless you make it so. Breathe and relax as God/Source dismantles every existing construct and belief system that has served as limitations. Align with the truth of wholeness and completeness. Merge with the light. Feel the warm nourishing elixir raise your awareness. You can't heal and expand when you begin from brokenness. By aligning with the truth of peace, abundance, health, and love, this will become your reality. You want to begin where you mean to end. If you want peace, then embody the vibration of Peace. If you want abundance, be abundant. Realize all the things to be grateful for. If you want love, realize that who you are is Love.

Ask to be free of everything within that keeps you trapped in the false belief of brokenness and the collateral limitations that resulted from this. Sit in stillness in the eye of the storm.

Day 9

Aligning with Life

There is a time for everything. A time of action and a time of rest. The rhythms of the days and nights, seasons, years and decades give evidence to this cosmic interchange. Every breath we take, inhaling and exhaling, is a representation of life's divine dance. As you stand before the ocean, you cannot help but feel the grandiose of creation. And just as there is a rhythm in the tides of the ocean there is a rhythm within your own body, your own life, and in your relationships to everyone and everything.

With this understanding one can relax into their life experiences. Rhythm is reflected everywhere. In business there are times of growth, plenty, decline, pauses, followed by more activity or decline. Adaptation to the ever -changing cycle of things creates new growth and the cycle repeats. Clinging tight to past ways creates stagnation and blocks the flow of life. In this changing world everything is subject to building or to breaking down. We like to avoid the breakdown parts of our lives, yet only in the breaking down and release can space be provided for newness to come in.

Embrace the time of action doing the best you have to offer, and equally embrace your time of rest. In doing so a sacred balance is achieved. Life will become an effortless flow as you allow life's rhythms to carry you.

Take a moment and notice how you respond to the rhythms in your life. When you are faced with a busy schedule do you feel anxious? Does your mind wander from the present moment to the list of things needed accomplished in the future? When the phone stops ringing, and your schedule book looks sparse do you worry? Do you welcome the interlude? If it helps for clarity write down the answers to these questions in a journal.

Day 10

Did you stop Dreaming?

Follow your dreams and the universe will open doors for you where there were once walls. The larger percentage of people dream of such things as increased abundance, freedom, a soul mate love relationship, a leaner fit body. In the hopes of achieving such things they attend workshops, and they buy a lot of books. Lindsay Myers, MBA, MPII in her article 'The Self Improvement Industry' states, "Self-improvement represents a $10 billion per year industry in the U.S. alone. In addition to high revenues, self-help also has a high recidivism rate, with the most likely purchaser of a self-help book being the same person who purchased one already in the last 18 months." (15) Lindsay Myers research revealed, "The origins of the self-help genre have been attributed to Victorian phrenologist George Combe's The Constitution of Man (1828), followed by Ralph Waldo Emerson's Compensation. Dale Carnegie, famous for his books How to Win Friends and Influence People (1936) and How to Stop Worrying and Start Living still holds a top-ranking spot on Amazon.com to this day." (16).

But what about the person that doesn't really know what they want? There are quizzes designed to help reveal what one is most passionate about. Questions include variations of, what is your purpose? What drives you? What inspires you? If you could be and do anything for the rest of your life, what would it be? Having a purpose in life can be the difference between achieving success or not. Successful people know what they want, why they want it, and how to make it happen.

The people who are not considered successful, the ones who are just getting by, often don't aim to do better. Perhaps they lack the confidence or have limiting self-beliefs. Sometimes life circumstances have left an indelible mark on their soul. The allure of success has no attraction. When one is experiencing grief or depression, chronic pain, or poor health the energy needed to even dream of a better future is nonexistent. These low vibrating states make it very challenging and cloud one's mind. Over time one gives up. This is not the same as surrendering.

If this has happened to you know that it is never too late for something new to emerge. The journey to a new life begins with a single step. When you drive a car across the country you don't have to see all the way to your destination. Rather you look at the road and paved white lines directly in front of you. There are signs along the way that point to your desired destination. The GPS navigation system gives directions and re-routes when needed.

Imagining the result is considered the most effective way toward achieving one's goal. However, when you have no idea as to what that looks like for you, asking you to hold such an image would be pointless. So, what do you do when you have been called into the desert? Recognize that the interlude between the life you once had and the new life that wants to emerge can be experienced as drawn out and wearisome. Use this time as a respite. Rest in the eye of your storms. Align with the highest vibration of love and abundance that you can imagine. Ask, what is the vibration and feeling of happiness?

Everyday do at least two things that move your life forward. It can be as simple as doing the dishes or cleaning out one drawer. Update your resume, explore new jobs for ten minutes. Think like an athlete and go to an exercise class. Read something inspirational. Meditate or connect with nature, even if it is pausing and observing your breath for two minutes. A friend told me that whenever she felt overwhelmed, depressed or discouraged she would set a timer for five minutes. She knew she could commit to five minutes. For five minutes, she would do something productive such as wash the dishes or organize her desk. Sometimes just taking the first few steps is all that is needed. This may be a dark lonely period marked with hardship, but it is temporary. Take the steps daily and let God/Source handle the rest. The emergence of a new life is assured. Every time one sits still in meditation and communes with the Divine their vibrational set point is raised. The higher your vibration, the more light you will be able to hold. This results in an easier manifestation of the life that you desire.

Today consciously do the things that you know will move your life forward. Pause and sit in stillness, so that you hear your inner guidance is a good start. Even better, act today.

Day 11

The Chrysalis

Butterflies earn their wings through great effort. The process of change is often painful because it is never without loss and sacrifices. If you are to transform beyond one form to another, a part of yourself needs to die. Letting go is not easy especially when you are used to thinking in a certain way about your life and how you live it. Just as a caterpillar dies so that a butterfly can be born, release your old ideas and embrace a necessary change so you can live an abounding life. Release the dream that no longer serves you. Step away from that relationship that is draining your life force. You will be amazed that when you establish new boundaries a renewed vitality will begin to emerge within you. Start new healthy habits. Despite your fears accept when it is a transformational time for you. In letting go of personal or professional relationships, a certain degree of loss is usually felt. When confronted with real change sometimes a person will contract back to a familiar way of living. It is easier to live out a pattern that is stagnant or painful because it is known. One can more effectively deal with and react to what they know than what they don't. Dealing with change brings up issues of trust. People don't embrace change because they don't trust. When one doesn't trust they cling to plans that aren't working, stick to routes that are obstructed, and obsess of relationships that aren't fulfilling. Real change requires one to take a leap into the unknown. Trust that what you cannot yet see is made manifested for a life that is in harmony with your evolution.

When you do embrace change and you are working on yourself spiritually and following your dreams you may continue to face constrictions. The financial picture still looks precarious. After working out for six months your body still holds the extra weight. Even though you signed up for E Harmony the person that matches your "list" hasn't been revealed. You may become discourage by what appears to be lack of progress.

Reference.com describes the cocooning of a caterpillar; "Once a caterpillar becomes a chrysalis, it may remain in that state for 10 days to 2 years. The time varies by species and the season in which the chrysalis is formed. Those that are formed in the fall usually do not become mature butterflies until spring." (17) Like the caterpillar confines itself, we experience darkness before the dawn. It may not appear that much is happening outwardly, but inner transformation is creating a new foundation for your life.

You are half way through a 21-day process. If you feel discourage, surrender. Have the willingness to trust in the unknown. Don't be in such a hurry to reach your desired destination. That way of thinking and longing pulls you out of this moment. The now moment is where the power of manifestation occurs. Affirm that Providence has a divine plan for you.

Today contemplate "not knowing". Affirm that you trust in the mystery of a Divine plan. Ask if your personal plan is in alignment with the Divine Plan for your life. If it isn't, then ask what Divine Will wants for you. Be still, so that you hear the answer.

Day 12

Pillar of Light

Realistically, having an upbeat happy disposition is impossible to maintain 24/7 for most people on this planet. I first came across the acronym H.A.L.T. when I was dating a chemical dependency counselor. H.A.L.T. stands for Hungry, Angry, Lonely, and Tired. Each one or any combination of these four increases the possibility of relapse. When you feel tense, dissatisfied, and weary, pause and check in with yourself. In these moments one is more likely to reach for unhealthy distractions, say things they will later regret, or purchase items they can't afford.

Most everyone is exhausted from the demands of life. Our mental reaction to life bears the fruits of stress and eventual burnout. We as a collective are saturated daily with input, much of which is extremely stressful to our bodies, minds and hearts. Life is moving so fast that we are unaware. We are unaware because we have not taken the time to be still and know. Before you attempt to adopt a new mind set it would be helpful to find a quiet place and practice a visualization. Visualizations along with slowing down and expanding your breathing will restore inner balance.

Visualize all tension falling away with each exhale. Inhale pure Divine nourishing light. Imagine a pillar of absolute strength running from the earth through the soles of your feet up through the top of your head, connecting you to the universe. Know that this pillar supports and strengthens you in any situation. You are nourished by the earth herself. It is important to reestablish balance within, daily. Life challenges can and do knock us off center. When we are off center, we are more likely to make decisions that are not the best.

Additionally, the negative behaviors of others can more easily penetrate our fields resulting in significant energy drain. Establishing and maintaining a strong inner core by aligning with the earth and God/Source is the most important thing to do daily.

Right now, as you read these words visualize a pillar of light coming down from the heavens and up from the center of the earth and into your body. See and feel this light expanding and filling your entire body until every cell is lit up with this powerful radiance. Observe the light illuminating and healing every aspect of your life.

Day 13

No more Excuses

Our minds can give us rational reasons for us not to do something. Yet what appears as pragmatic often inhibits our ability to reach our goals. Reexamine your excuses. Is there an alternative solution before you give up or say; "I will begin that task tomorrow"? Most people make excuses because they don't want to take responsibility for their choices. Sometimes one has a fear of communicating honestly in certain situations. Rather than authentically expressing their choice or saying no, they give excuses and tell others what they want to hear to avoid conflict. This way of being expresses a victim mentality, and the consequences are a disempowered energy. When you take 100% responsibility for all the choices you make in life you then have the power to make the changes you desire. You are no longer at the whims of outside influences.

Who you are is your word. When you are out of integrity in any way with what you speak, you diminish your ability to create in life. Words and thoughts are very powerful so be mindful. When you are asked for a financial donation and you use the excuse that you can't afford it, you have created and attracted lack and limitation into your life. You have the right to simply just say No. The same holds true pretending to not feel well because you don't want to go to that graduation party. Superficially those excuses seem to make things easier, but in the quantum field the untruths diminish your power to create and manifest the life you desire. This isn't a conversation about morality rather understand that there are fundamental laws that direct this physical paradigm. Living in integrity and taking responsibility for all your thoughts, and choices will yield positive results. Making excuses directs one down the victim alley. By committing to our priorities, taking responsibility for all our choices, and communicating honestly to others, there will be no need for excuses. Living a life of integrity entrains one with the flow of abundance.

Where are you making excuses or blaming others for your current realities presentation? What are you putting off for tomorrow that could be done today? Lovingly make a self-inquiry.

Day 14

Having a Breakdown

It is the nature of all things to eventually breakdown. Such endings are necessary for something new to be born. Having a breakdown is often the catharsis that is needed to keep our emotional life in balance. Most of us have had the experience of holding back our emotions for such a long period of time that when they finally come out, we have something resembling a breakdown. For a certain time, the overwhelming flood of feelings coursing through our bodies consumes us, and we stop functioning. Often, these outbursts take us by surprise, welling up within us as we drive to or from work, watching a movie, or engaged in some otherwise mundane task. We may feel like we do not know what triggered us, or if we do know, it does not make sense of our overpowering emotional response. This is because we are releasing feelings that have accumulated over a long period of time, and whatever inspired the release was just a catalyst for a much needed catharsis.

My daughter showed me a short video of her 2-year-old daughter having her first full blown temper tantrum. My granddaughter was thoroughly enraged. Her tiny little body had reached critical capacity and she released the emotions. The next moment she was happy again. As I watched my sweet happy granddaughter wail with magnanimous intensity I realized that same scream was raging inside of me. I however, held the intense emotions in check. A part of me was concerned if I let it out the neighbors would come running over to see what was wrong. Another part felt that if I started releasing the scream it would never end. Finally, on the anniversary of my son's death, I sat in my car in the garage with the door closed and wailed the sounds only expressed from a mother who lost her child.

It is human instinct after any experience of pain to shield the self from future hurt. Anguished emotions are often repressed. Unexpressed emotions manifest as physical distress. Holding emotions in is very detrimental to the physical body. Headaches, a tight neck, a chronic cough, anxiety, exhaustion, high blood pressure are only a few of the numerous symptoms from unexpressed emotions.

The good news is eventually something or someone will trigger repressed emotions. When we find ourselves during such an experience, it is important that we allow it to happen, rather than fight it or try to shut down. Wherever we are, we can try to find a private, safe place in which to let our feelings out. If we cannot access such a place immediately, we can promise to set aside some time for ourselves at our earliest possible convenience, perhaps taking a day off work. The important thing is that we need to give our emotional system some much-needed attention. It is essential that we allow ourselves to release the pent-up emotions inside ourselves so that they do not create imbalances in our bodies and minds.

When you are feeling better, plan to find a way to process your emotions more regularly. You can do this by employing a therapist or making a regular date to talk to a trusted friend. Journaling can also be a great way to acknowledge and release your emotions, as can certain forms of meditation. Making room in your life for tending to your emotions on a regular basis will keep you healthy and balanced. Turn within and realign with Divinity. Cultivate a daily routine to meditate and visualize your body, mind and emotions returned to balance.

Today take a few minutes. Sit down and place your hands over your heart. Feel your feet on the surface below. Visualize a connection to the earth. Feel the life force energy flowing up from the earth into your feet. Visualize this elixir moving up through and saturating your entire body. With consistent practice you will feel stronger and stronger currents of earth energy moving through your form.

Now draw your awareness upward to above your head. Feel the loving light of Divinity flowing into your crown and illuminating your body. With this platform of light as your support structure draw your attention to your emotions, especially the ones sitting just below the surface. Call them forward to the embrace of love. Feel your feelings. Be honest with yourself. Allow the emotions to reveal the truth about how you really feel about certain situations. Pay attention to the hopes and desires that have been repressed. Feel the release of tears streaming down your face. The most powerful person is one who lives in complete harmony with their self. To be in harmony is to accept 100% of all that you are. Emotions are energies in motion. They want to move and often one represses emotions because they don't want to feel. It is safe to feel.

Allow whatever arises to flow through you.

Day 15

Running on Empty

There are times in our lives when it seems our bodies are running on empty. We are not sick, nor are we necessarily pushing ourselves to the limit-- rather, the energy we typically enjoy has mysteriously dissipated, leaving only fatigue. Many people grow accustomed to feeling this way because they do not know that it is possible to exist in any other state. The body's natural state, however, is one of energy, clarity, and balance. Cultivating these three virtues in our own bodies is a balancing act that we must work on daily. It is crucial to develop a refined awareness of the self and then make appropriate changes based on our observations.

A few moments of self-awareness in which you take inventory of your daily schedule, and personal choices made will help you to identify what is causing your depletion. If you are struggling with an overfull agenda, prioritization is important. Other possible factors include diet or an underlying illness.

Coping with and healing physical depletion will be easier when you accept that the underlying cause might be more complex than you at first imagined. A harried lifestyle or a deficient diet may represent only one part of a larger issue affecting your mood and exhausted state.

Emotions have a huge effect and impact on the physical body. Unresolved grievances of the mind and heart do take their toll on your physical self. It requires a lot of corporeal energy to process intense emotions. Conversely, emotional states of grief and depression leave you feeling lethargic and often exhausted.

Ultimately you are in control of how you feel. However, it takes consistent practice and discipline to reside in higher positive vibrational states. Daily visual meditations are useful tools to reenergize and bring vitality back.

A still pond will perfectly mirror back whatever is there. When a person becomes calm within, they can begin to perceive the world as it is and know what is going on in others around them. Today visualize a completely still pond or lake. Imagine your mind to be as clear and still as this body of water. Feel the clarity and spaciousness. Become absorbed in the Peace. Thoughts that emerge are simply ripples on the surface. Return to the image of a pristine still lake. Hold that imagine as your mind. Even if for a few moments, cultivate this practice daily.

Day 16

Turning Inward Meditation

It is helpful to use visualizations to restore balance and energy to you. I recommend you read and record this visualization meditation for yourself. There are free recording apps on cell phones. The sound of your own voice guiding you creates a deeper experience. When I have a busy day that is pulling me out of balance, I sit for a couple of minutes and listen to a recording of this meditation:

I turn away from the outer world that surrounds me to enter the inner world of my being. As I do I focus in on the clear space in the undisturbed center where a great power exists within me. This is the very power that creates universes. This power lives within me at the very heart and center of consciousness within myself. This universal intelligence mind/spirit is working through all levels of my being, mentally, emotionally, physically and throughout the entire matrix of me. This primal light Christ like energy is vibrating through every nerve, cell, tissue and molecule of my body. Through my energy field both outwardly and inwardly.

Every internal organ of my body is at its core a vibrational field of energy. And all the energy fields that comprise my body are subject to the great power primal energy of the universal holy light, pure mind/ God/infinite intelligence. This light is entering the nucleus of every cell of my body and as it does, it begins to adjust the rhythms and energy frequencies contained within my energy matrix of every one of the billions of cells that make up my form. As this occurs all is reestablished into Divine Harmony with the Divine design by which my body mind and soul was created to function perfectly. If there is any part of my body or mind that is out of alignment with the perfect design of the universe for perfect health, right here right now, those energies are being adjusted to the rhythm and motions of perfect harmony as God/Nature intended for me. my body and state of polarity, balance and harmony is established. I now breathe in rhythm with the harmony of the planets as they move through their orbits.

I as a finite expression of the infinite know that I am the cosmic presence of the universe. I live in power because power lives in me. All my trauma/karma is dissolved into the primal light energy that is the 1st cause of the universe. My body is entrained to Divine harmony, wholeness and completeness. My body is a temple of the infinite and eternal. This is the creative process of the universe that men call God. The entirety of my body is bathed, soothed, caressed in the gentle loving care of Spirit. I am refreshed and renewed, and I give Thanks and so it is.

Day 17

Contemplate Oneness

We interact with the world in a dualistic fashion. We even make moralistic judgments with our opinions, and attitudes about other people. We declare some people to be just like us and others to be different. The ones that are different we frequently declare to be wrong. Often a person's beliefs and values are so cemented that they are convinced that their way is the only way. Yet from a polarized point of view they can't perceive that there could be alternative vantage points. The average person uses their basic five senses as a display panel for which they perceive and formulate their world view. Their personal beliefs created from previous experiences are filters which inhibit the true actual reality. We only know a fractional segment of the whole. All the while a kaleidoscope of patterns intersect meeting into absolute Oneness.

Science has discovered that the universe we exist in is holographic in nature. This means that the whole is contained within a single part. For example, if you slice a piece of fruit into sections the entire hologram of the whole fruit is contain within each slice. The DNA matrix blueprint for your entire body is contained within each individual cell. Contemplate for a moment the seed of a tree. The entire everything that makes up a tree including the years of growth of the tree, is contained within one tiny seed. The perfect pattern of wholeness is and always has been here.

There is a unified field which extends itself through the relative scalar dimensions of the space-time manifold to gaze back at the complexity of its own creation through the eyes of sentient beings. This doesn't conclude that humans are more important, conscious, or alive than anything else in the universe. Consciousness expresses itself through all things by means of a fractal-holographic information field, creating a singular reality observed from an infinitude of creative perspectives, all which contribute to the Whole.

It is the nature of the mind to separate the life experience into an individual on the inside of the human body perceiving the other- outside world. This results in a partial one-sided life experience. This what the Bible refers to in the first book Genesis when Adam and Eve ate of the fruit of the tree of knowledge. When Adam and Eve covered their nakedness, their souls took on the form of a physical human body. The light wave discussed in science then became a particle. The light became encased in form. Human form was created and with it the cycle of life and death. The play of opposites since the "fall of man" makes up the matrix of our world. It is very important to understand though that the disconnection is internal in the mind's perception, and as such inhibits a person from knowing true oneness.

Contemplate and give strong consideration, to your perception of self. Your sense of self, and continuity of experience is not contained within anything in your brain, or body in any physical way. The cells of your body die and all the material that makes the physical you are replaced continuously throughout your life. Yet there is a you that continues to exist. Whether in a two-year-old body, or in a 56-year-old body, it is the same you. It is Consciousness that remains constant, thus giving you the life experience. Let go of who you think you are. Who you are is "this moment". Meditate on the statement, "Who I am is this moment."

Day 18
The Space Between

What seems like empty space around us is very much alive and intricately structured. The space between is not dead space, even though at one time scientists believed that it was. A medium must exist to transmit signals from one place to another. We take for granted that our TV's, cell phones, and laptop computers turn on and work as they do. We give little thought that there is a medium which connects our devices to the towers. What we perceive as space is a field of energy. This energy appears everywhere in all moments and has existed from the beginning of time. This connecting matrix is Love, it is God, Divine Source. The Bible discourses that God is omnipresent. This means God is everywhere, always. Jesus taught that "the kingdom of God is within". Therefore, a logical conclusion is You are everywhere, always. Not the identity as you that you created, the You that is unbounded, eternal, and free. Everything in this physical world including the physical you as you know yourself to be is simply a projection of God/Source/Consciousness. Many religious texts specifically in Christianity discourse on surrendering thy will to God's will. In Hinduism and Buddhism, the sutras and texts teach on the dissolution of the individual self into the Divine absolute. Meditation is practiced for this purpose. The mind will resist releasing the individual self because from the minds perspective that would be death. To cease to exist is very troublesome. Here is the cosmic joke! The individual that is a separate limited you never existed in the first place. Therefore, death and ceasing to exist is impossible. The You that is Pure Consciousness was never born and will never die. It is very possible that the words you are reading here feel like a foreign language. It is probable that your mind will argue with these words. This is because your mind can no longer evolve you to where your soul is directing you.

Release your thoughts. Contemplate the inhalation and exhalation of breath for the lungs. This inward and outward movement, like the tides of the ocean is an expression of polarity. We are Spirit (God) in a continuous dynamic dance that constantly is moving into and out of physical form. The only limits in our lives, are the ones we believe in.

Today Say to yourself, "I am the Space in which my body and my entire life exists in." Contemplate that your soul isn't in your body rather your body is in your soul. Feel the spaciousness of that.

Day 19

Life is a Mirror

Every one of us feels a solitary sensation behind the fabric of our everyday lives. This is experienced as a longing that tugs at the heart. Your longing is the central core of every mystical path. The heartsickness of the lover is a longing to return to the source in which everything is embraced in its complete wholeness. Our suffering is the labor pain that awakens us to our higher consciousness. This is the space where love joins this world with the infinite and our hearts embrace life. For within the heart of oneness Love becomes life's deepest wonder.

Stop struggling and come into remembrance. Decide to embody the vibration of wholeness. Simply state, "Today I choose to embody the vibration and frequency of wholeness. When you start really loving yourself and vibrating wholeness the universe vibrates back to you this wholeness. Make the place of absolute Love the driving motivation by which you live your life. When you start from a place of Love you finish at a space of Love. The deepest part of you, when embraced allows the light to shine forth. The more we are anchored in Self-Love the greater Love is reflected in life's mirror. Your connection to soul/God is the most important thing you can do in your life. Everything else is a by-product.

Regardless of whom you are, or how you were raised; once you come into alignment with the powerful vibrational transformation of your inner spirit, your life will change in miraculous ways. Whatever it is that you want to see reflected to you, be that! If you want to experience Love, Be Love. If you want to experience health, set the intention to embody the frequency of health. If you want to experience abundance, look around you and feel gratitude for the gifts life has already offered you.

When you place an inquiry to the universe, an answer will be provided because Source answers the question. "Ask and you will receive" is a fundamental law of this paradigm, because the question creates a space for the Universe to come in and fill. Living in the question creates space for expansion to occur.

Today contemplate, "What is the Highest Frequency of me that I can embody at this time?" Ask the Universe to show you what is abundance. Ask to be shown what is love and happiness. How does it get any better than this? Learn to live in the question.

Day 20

Good, good, good Vibrations

The origin of creation is not the mind, or unconscious mind, it is the soul. There are no limitations here at this level of vibration. Shift happens through vibration. The elevation of frequency creates change. Where we vibrate is reflected in our outer experiences of our lives. Tap into the highest remembrance there is. Stop the endless seeking and searching outside and align with your soul. Instead of trying to fix and improve you, which is based on identity, tap into your soul, which is whole and complete. Live from this place of connection and all things are possible.

If you must work on yourself, work at the level of vibration, which is not shifting thoughts, rather shifting energy. When you reside in the space of Love, you will no longer accept your limited life.

It's time to stop existing and start living. Love yourself so profoundly, that you can access everything that you are.

Sit for a moment and imagine until you know that Divinity is flowing through every molecule of your body. Create for yourself a different orientation with your body, and with your life. Align your personal frequency to the vibration of pure Love absolute. Feel the radiance of this love that is your inner most nature. Be this love. When you embody the highest frequency, the rays of light naturally flow outward gifting and harmonizing the world around you. By holding this vibrational state as your new normal, shifts will begin to occur in your world. Doors open for you that do not normally open for others. At this higher vibrational pattern, you have a special quality and energy about you that others will want to gift to you, offer you jobs and opportunities.

This all starts with being the vibration of Love and dissolving that which is anything other than this. Today choose to be free of all inner trauma, fears and judgments. Let go of the reigns of control and turn the driving over to Providence. Honor all your feelings without trying to fix or figure them out. Do not worry, if there is something you need to identify, it most definitely will reveal itself to you. Bring your awareness back to your breath. By focusing on your breathing, you stop the mental chatter and realign your frequencies. Come into Love. Now stay there.

Day 21

Walk on Water

When we dialogue and converse with Divinity /God it is called prayer. When we experience revelation or inspiration from God it comes in different ways. Occasionally, though rarely, Divinity speaks to us instantly and dramatically. The conversion of St Paul through a blinding light is an example of a sudden, powerful transformational communication. These quick transcendental moments are like standing in a huge dark warehouse, then turning on the light switch. At first you may be blinded by the brightness, but soon after, you see everything in the warehouse clearly. Prior to turning the light switch on, you stumbled around in the dark. Dramatic events, near death experiences, or deep emotional experiences can immediately open the door for the light of God to come rushing in. In that moment, clarity often replaces naïve, and the purpose of your soul's true earth expression is revealed with volition.

Collectively we are in the midst of tumultuous storms. The concurrent dramas, wars, political duplicity, financial hardships, domestic and foreign violence have conditioned everyone into a fight or flight vibrational state. It is imperative to recognize that for every state that exists, the diametrically opposite exists as a potential. This means the darker and denser an event or condition is the exact opposite of pure bright light that is infinite is available in the same moment. At the surface we see all the wrongness, all the evil and ignorance, yet a revolution of awakening is being rapidly ushered in.

There is an infinite energy that lives inside of you. This Holy Light reveals itself when one withdraws from outer distractions. You will feel a pull beyond reason deep within the core of your being. Your soul unsatisfied and starving for purpose will pursue until you answer its call. Take the time today to withdraw from the outer world so you can begin to experience the authentic light and power of God that is pure Love. This invisible force of Divinity this truly unknowable source of Grace and benevolence is experienced in your life during your most vulnerable moments. This is because you have been broken open to receive. The experience of knowing, of becoming absorbed into the image and likeness of God is not something that can be grasp mentally. It is made real only when it is illuminated from within.

When the world is harsh become the opposite, not in resistance to the wrongness rather in compassion for the suffering born out of ignorance. Like a gentle morning sunrise align yourself with softness and the peace. Your journey into the eye of the storm is the distance of one choice. It is the choice to abide in Love. It is the choice to align with the highest luminosity. It is the choice to embody and hold the highest frequency of light available to this earth plane currently. The process is a daily commitment to be still and surrender.

Today and everyday choose to abide in Love by asking the question, "What would Love do?" Then silence your mind so that you hear the answer. When you lay down your sword, only then will the path of miracles appear before you.

It is then you can and will Walk on Water.

Chapter 7

Samadhi

Samadhi is a word used in Hinduism, Buddhism, Jainism, Sikhism and various yogic schools of thought to describe the ultimate stage of meditation. Samadhi is the complete absorption of the individual self into pure Divine Consciousness or God. In Christianity it is the state of Oneness Jesus refers to, "I and the Father are one" (John 10:30). Many Christian religious leaders interpret this statement as Jesus making the claim that he is equal to God. While I am not at all debating the truth of that interpretation, there is a fundamental flaw in this line of reasoning. To be One with God there cannot be two. You cannot be one with something and be separate from it.

One is one. To claim you are equal to something else indicates you hold a belief in separation. To be equal to something else there must be two; the you that is equal, and the other that you are equal too. Samadhi is the state in which the individual "I" which is actually your identity, is integrated into the Eternal "I" of God. Identity is how one views oneself both as a person and in relation to other people, ideas and nature. Identity is a mental construct used to describe yourself in relation to other. The message of Jesus is the dissolution of separation. In this dissolution the only state Jesus abides in is God. Jesus is God. In the gospel of John, a claim is made by Jesus that He is God. 'You do not know me or my Father,' Jesus replied. 'If you knew me, you would know my Father also'" (John 8:19) "'I tell you the truth,' Jesus answered, 'before Abraham was born, I am!'" (John 8:58). "I and the Father are one" (John 10:30).

The experience of oneness is remembered when you embody Divinity. When you realize that you are a vibrational being, then everything becomes possible. The God presence, the "I AM", is you, Separation does not exist, and it never did. You are unconditional love. This Love depends not on external factors, rather this Love emanates from within. You are joy, and peace. You are Sat- Chid-Ananda (the pure awareness of the eternal is Bliss). The conversion into this state of Being which is the actual true reality cannot be achieved through your mind. Your thoughts can not take you there. The experience of the totality of Being is given in moments of Grace. Your job is to show up and surrender daily. Ask yourself this very important question. "What am I before my thoughts and memories?" You will notice a Gap or space in response to that question. However, the mind doesn't know what to do with the clear space and silence. Therefore, it will fill up again with thoughts based on memories of who you know yourself to be. Therefore, if you want to wake up and end this cycle of suffering, a daily practice of silence and aligning with Divinity is crucial.

You are not who you were yesterday, seven days ago, or a year ago, yet you still relate to yourself as a former aspect of yourself. This means, you relate to a you, that is a memory of you, instead of who you are in the moment. When you awaken every day and look in the mirror. Do you abide in the judgment of you, or the acceptance of you? Do you compare yourself to others, or what the media wants you to believe is acceptable, and successful life station? On so many levels, we have been programmed to strive, and to achieve in areas that are fleeting, and superficial. The only true lasting fulfillment is an eternal state of Being, which is this moment of Presence that is born of contentment, and harmony. You are part of something far greater, and this greater source is leading you into a greater expression, and higher truth. You are a spark of eternity. You are an expression of Divinity.

Most people are sleep walking through life. They relate to everyone and everything at the surface level. People are afraid to feel into the fullness of the ache, into what lies beneath. Do not be afraid. You are the space in which everything arises. Trust in you, for through Divinity you are stronger than your human mind can conceive.

Be still and feel your feelings. Expand your awareness and release whatever is keeping you stuck in victimhood. Feel the tears you will not shed. Notice a tight pressure, sometimes as a vise-like grip around your throat. Observe a shallow breathing, or chronic cough. Feel the butterflies, or nausea in your stomach. Acknowledge the deep,

deep sadness, or perhaps a knife in your heart. Cry out from the center of your being. Embrace the hot bitter tears staining your face, for soon they will cool, and flow in a welcome release. Allow yourself to let go. Allow yourself to dissolve. The tug, the sadness, the ache, is a knock at the door. On the other side is your awakening to a new life.

You cannot make enlightenment happen. You cannot control the process of awakening. What you can and must do is prepare the soil and plant the seeds. It is important to give water and sun light. Samadhi is given through Grace.

God is omnipresent. God is everywhere and is everything. Therefore, when you release and surrender your individual self (which is just a mental construct) to God/Divinity you are everything and everywhere. Your soul knows this as truth. Your mind most likely will hold onto your separate individual expression.

Take a moment right now and check in with yourself. Are you present, or are you distracted by other concerns? Your life is meant to be felt in the fullness of each moment, that arises. Yet often, people dis-associate from their own lives. They turn to distractions or seek to numb their emotions. When triggered, or during grief, people turn to social media. When they are angry, or insecure, they run to the refrigerator in search for a snack. When they feel scared, or are bored, they turn to alcohol, drugs, or sex. All these distractions inhibit one's ability to authentically live. Why do we distract ourselves? Because to embrace each moment requires the willingness to be available for everything that is moving through us. Just allow every moment to arise in your awareness. Be completely with what is, regardless if the emotions are happy, or sad.

We hold onto the good feelings and resist the bad ones. Both approaches perpetuate suffering, because of attachment, or wanting experiences to be different than they are.

There is only one field of consciousness. The perfect pattern of wholeness is and has always been here. Stop resisting your life, cease reaching for a distraction when an emotion arises that is not to your liking. When you simply are with what is, you will realize that you are a vibrational being. To vibrate means the action of motion of movement. You, and your life, are movements flowing from one experience to the next. When you fully align with this truth, everything becomes possible.

The repeated emersion of Divine connection through meditation forms imprints as your heart mind and emotions harmonize into Transcendental Consciousness.

The repeated moments of Samadhi which is the fruit of your meditation practice establishes experiences of liberation and unification. Over time this will become your primary reference point for your life.

Each time you experience the Light of God move through you, the dense stuck heavy content that has been tethering your life dissolves more and more. Stop chasing after the world attempting to shift your outer experiences. Trying to change others and situations yields very limited results. Go within and abide in the state of Pure Divine Presence. This is a vibrational practice. When you shift your energy, your life will shift. Divine absorption is the solution to everything. Surrendering to the Absolute aligns you with abundance, even though this world was designed to operate from fear, scarcity, and limitation.

If you make a genuine commitment to a daily practice of sitting in stillness and asking for God's Grace; over time, Samadhi will be all there is. This is both the journey and the goal.

Instead of running in a circle seeking to complete karmic cycles of incompletion, your reality will begin to reflect the cycle of completion. Ultimately the choice is yours. Daily emersion with Divinity clears and harmonizes the past. Once the past is cleared and you stop living into the past, you will no longer be burdened by the imprints of the past. Free from the past the pure light of Source can express through you unencumbered.

When you are connected to God and 100% vibrationally aligned to Divinity you are connected to all things. Therefore, lack and limitation are impossible. We experience separation, lack and limitation because we have edited and filtered out Divinity. God has been taught as a separate Being existing in a separate place often described as a heavenly one up in the clouds. The only separation occurring is in the mind's viewpoint. Come back to this space. Live in and vibrate Pure Presence. Shift your reference point from separation to unity.

The world is going to continue to spin around you in patterns of chaos. You cannot step away from the world because the world that you see is born out of your own perceptions. That is why two people who are at the same event can, and often do have different experiences of that event. The event itself is neutral.

I love dogs. All my memories of having dogs as pets are happy ones. I went for a walk with a friend. We both saw a dog walking with their person. I felt happy inside. I said Hi to the dog and ask their person if I could pet the dog.

My friend had the experience as a child of getting bit by a dog. The trauma of that incident imprinted her nervous system resulting in a fear of all dogs. When she saw the same dog walking with their person, anxiety and trepidation immediately arose in her. My friend's reaction was opposite of mine because her past experiences with dogs were negative.

The world is simply whatever it is. Collectively as expressed in news reports, through Facebook, and Twitter feeds, we are bombarded with information; most which is chaotic, and fear based.

There is a different reality available to you. In the Bible, Luke 17:20–21, Jesus says, "The kingdom of God does not come with observation; nor will they say, 'See here!' or 'See there!' For indeed, the kingdom of God is within you" (NKJV).

Most people oscillate between reacting and arguing against what they feel is wrong and displaying avoidance behavior. They live in quiet desperation waiting for a promise of heaven after this physical incarnation is over.

Don't wait until your life is over for happiness and peace. Reacting and arguing against the other adds to the hurricane. Instead of focusing on what is wrong, look for what can be made right. If you must Be anything, Be the solution.

Lay down the grievances of your past. Pick up a new resolve. Step out of the boat, and release everything that has tethered you. Carry Love, forgiveness, and courage in your heart. Take my hand and walk with me into the eye of the storm. Rest in a Peace that surpasses all understanding.

I dwell in the mystery of the great unknown, fluid, beautiful and free.

I dance with the wind, and relish each breath, ecstatic each day just to be.

I sing with the joy of the planets and stars

I laugh with the waves and the sea.

For I am Spirit forever unfolding, unbonded, eternal, and free.

(Author unknown)

Works Cited

1. http://newtheologicalmovement.blogspot.com/2011/08/walking-on-water-spiritual-meaning-of.html
2. https://www.bing.com/search/stuck
3. www.princes-trust.org.uk/about-the-trust/news-views/the-princes-trust-2018-macquarie-youth-index
4. https://www.nps.gov/subjects/cherryblossom/bloom-watch.htm
5. https://www.livescience.com/28499-cold-spring-cherry-blossom-delay.html
6. https://www.scientificamerican.com/article/caterpillar-butterfly-metamorphosis-explainer
7. https://www.sciencedaily.com/releases/2015/03/150330112236.htm
8. https://www.healthline.com/health/eeg
9. John 6: 18-21, Holy Bible, New International Version (NIV), Copyright 2011-2017
10. https://www.equilibrium-e3.com/images/PDF/The%20Research%20of%20Candace%20Pert.pdf
11. vibesup.com/blog/
12. Matthew 14:22-23, Holy Bible, New International Version (NIV), Copyright 2011-2017
13. http://alcoholrehab.com/addiction-recovery/one-day-at-a-time-in-recovery
14. https://personalexcellence.co/blog/21-day-trial
15. ttps://articles.mercola.com/.../15/neuroplasticity-brain-health.aspx
16. Holy Bible, New Revised Standard Version. New York: Oxford UP, 1989. Print

---

17. http://ww2010.atmos.uiuc.edu/%28Gh%29/guides/mtr/hurr/stages/cane/eye.rxml
18. Quote from Annemarie
19. https://en.wikipedia.org/wiki/Paradoxical_intention
20. https://thisimperfectjourney.wordpress.com/2012/03/18/acceptance
21. https://en.wikipedia.org/wiki/Culture
22. Holy Bible, New International Version, Copyright 2011-2017 Biblical
23. http://brainblogger.com/2014/05/23/the-self-help-industry-helps-itself-to-billions-of-dollars/
24. http://citation.allacademic.com/meta/p_mla_apa_research_citation/0/9/0/8/7/pages90873/p90873-1.php
25. https://www.reference.com/pets-animals/long-caterpillar-stay-chrysalis-96933dc39d351e16
26. https://www.merriam-webster.com/dictionary/identity
27. Grimes, Jeanie. I Painted the Light: Using Spirituality to Heal from Childhood Sexual Abuse. Balboa Press. 2013. Print.
28. Numbers 3: 1-36, Holy Bible, New Living Translation, Copyright 1996,2004,2007
29. https://science.howstuffworks.com/science-vs-myth/extrasensory-perceptions/numerology.htm
30. Green, Glenda. Love Without End – Jesus Speaks. Spiritis Publishing, Copyright 1999-2006
31. http://www.dimension1111.com/7-universal-laws-the-hermetic-principles.html
32. John 17, Holy Bible, New International Version (NIV), Copyright 2011-2017

About the Author

Dr. Daria Kathleen Sherman PhD is an internationally recognized contemporary spiritual teacher. Through immediate transmission and ongoing training, she guides people to a deeper level of self-awareness, and healing. Her associates and clients value her special gift for seeing deeply into others, along with her capacity in supporting others in revealing, applying, and practically expressing their inner truth free from limitations created from trauma. Her focus is on both personal transcendence and an active engagement with the global challenges facing humanity in today's postmodern world. Daria teaches and trains groups in stress management, and movement re-education. She is a motivational speaker and the author of 29 published books. Daria holds a doctorate in Philosophy specializing in metaphysical counseling. Daria is trained in Conflict Analysis and Interfaith Conflict Resolution by the United States Institute of Peace International Programs Education and Training Center. She has specialized training in Living with grief. Daria completed Qigong healing training, and she is a Certified Practitioner for Psychophysical Integration and Movement Education. A traditional Reiki master teacher and a licensed Medical Massage Therapist Daria has worked with thousands of clients over the years and has developed her own method of Healing Touch and Soul Biology Healing.

heartlandhealer@mail.com

www.dariasherman.com